T0178770

QUEER CHAMELEON
AND FRIENDS

Amee Wilson is a British–Australian illustrator and writer with a love of creativity for good.

Born in the UK, she has recently returned after six years working in Australia and currently lives in London with her partner.

By day, Amee works as an Art Director in advertising with a passion for ideas that tackle inequality. By night, she illustrates and animates the Queer Chameleon and Anxious Animals series. *Queer Chameleon and Friends* is her first publication.

♪ @queeeerchameleon

◎ @queeeerchameleon

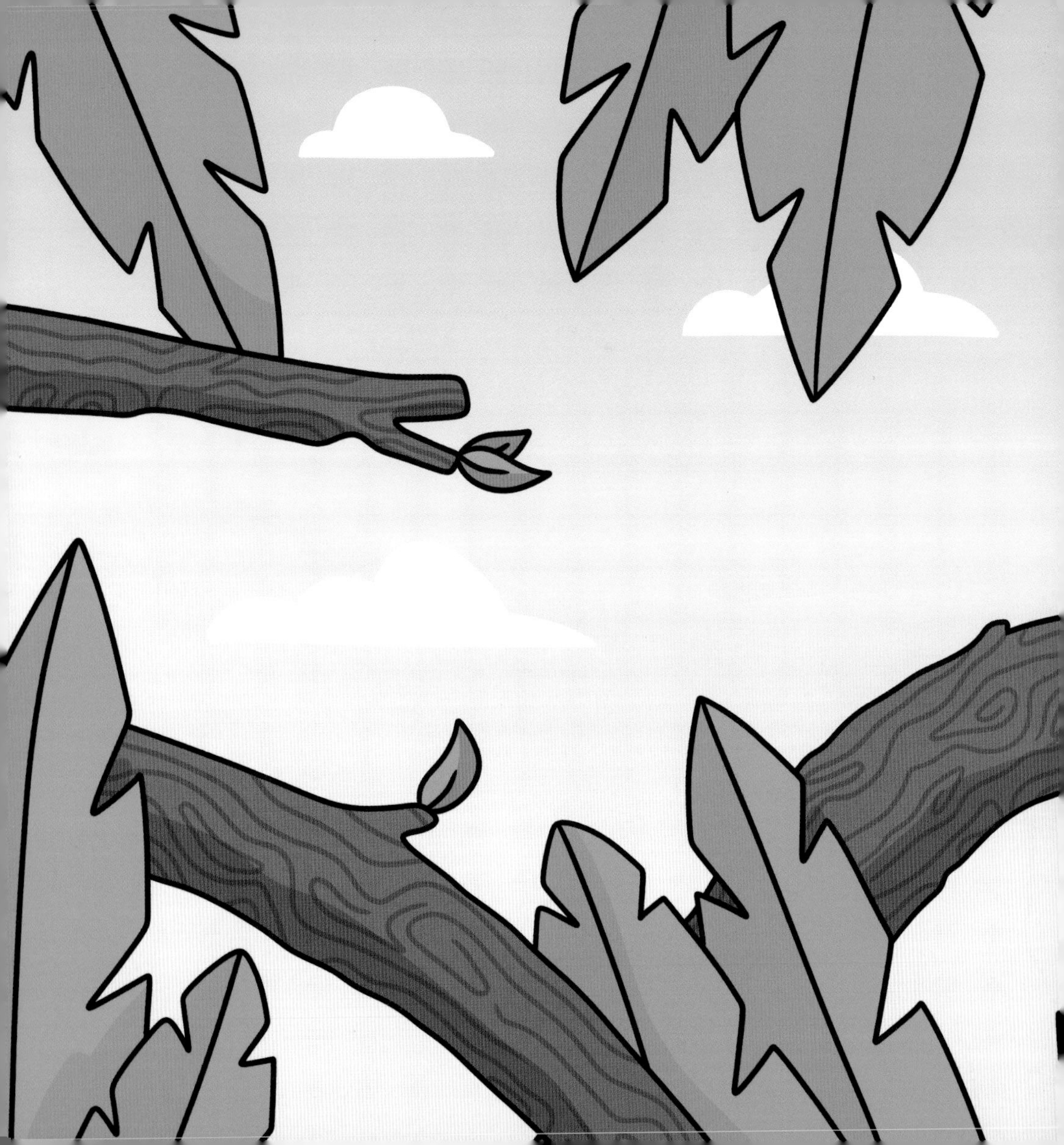

QUEER
CHAMELEON

AND FRIENDS

WRITTEN & ILLUSTRATED
BY AMEE WILSON

EBURY PRESS

UK | USA | Canada | Ireland | Australia
India | New Zealand | South Africa | China

Ebury Press is part of the Penguin Random House group of companies
whose addresses can be found at global.penguinrandomhouse.com

Penguin
Random House
Australia

First published by Ebury Press, 2023
Text and illustrations copyright © Amee Wilson, 2023
The moral right of the author has been asserted.

Cover design and illustrations by Amee Wilson
Internal design by Adam Laszczuk © Penguin Random House Australia Pty Ltd
Printed and bound in China by 1010 Printing International

A catalogue record for this
book is available from the
National Library of Australia

ISBN 978 1 76134 017 8

penguin.com.au

We at Penguin Random House Australia acknowledge that Aboriginal and Torres Strait Islander
peoples are the Traditional Custodians and the first storytellers of the lands on which we live and work.
We honour Aboriginal and Torres Strait Islander peoples' continuous connection to Country, waters,
skies and communities. We celebrate Aboriginal and Torres Strait Islander stories, traditions and
living cultures; and we pay our respects to Elders past and present.

CONTENTS

Hey Frens!

Back in 2021, Queer Chameleon started as a webcomic about being part of the LGBTQ+ community. And geez, well, it's grown into something I could never have expected.

It's led to me connecting and collaborating with other LGBTQ+ creators, learning so much more about identity, broadening into animation and connecting with millions of you around the world along the way. And now look at us . . . meeting in the pages of an ACTUAL BOOK. Who would've thunk it? Definitely not me! It's a joy to bring this to you. Thank you to my long-time supporters and if you're totally new . . . Hi! Hello! How exciting!

If you're wondering 'why chameleons?' or 'what do all the colours mean?' . . . I thought they were the perfect animal to represent and celebrate the broad spectrum of sexual, romantic and gender identities. While chameleons are known for using their colour-changing ability to blend into their surroundings, the characters in this book use it to stand out. Wearing the colours of different pride flags, Queer Chameleon and their friends represent a range of labels. There's a guide in the opening chapter to help identify them all.

The remaining chapters are filled with comics about the ridiculousness of a world not always designed for us while exploring such topics as: coming out (or not), awkward-but-sometimes-accurate clichés and 'beyond binary' thinking. Online fans may recognise some familiar favourites. I've also created nearly sixty brand new comics just for this book.

Some comics I created to make you laugh, some to educate and others simply to give you the warm fuzzies. Of course, some might not resonate with you at all. Everyone's experience in this broad community of ours is completely unique and personal.

No matter your take, I hope this book helps bridge gaps and create understanding both inside and outside our community. Because, above all, *Queer Chameleon and Friends* is intended to make people feel seen, validated and loved. I have learned so much while creating this work – I hope we can continue to laugh and learn together!

Thank you for being here, you wonderful human bean. Please enjoy this random little book of colourful reptiles.

Amee

CHAPTER 1

WHAT THE FLAG?!

Get to know Queer Chameleon and friends
and the meaning behind their stripes

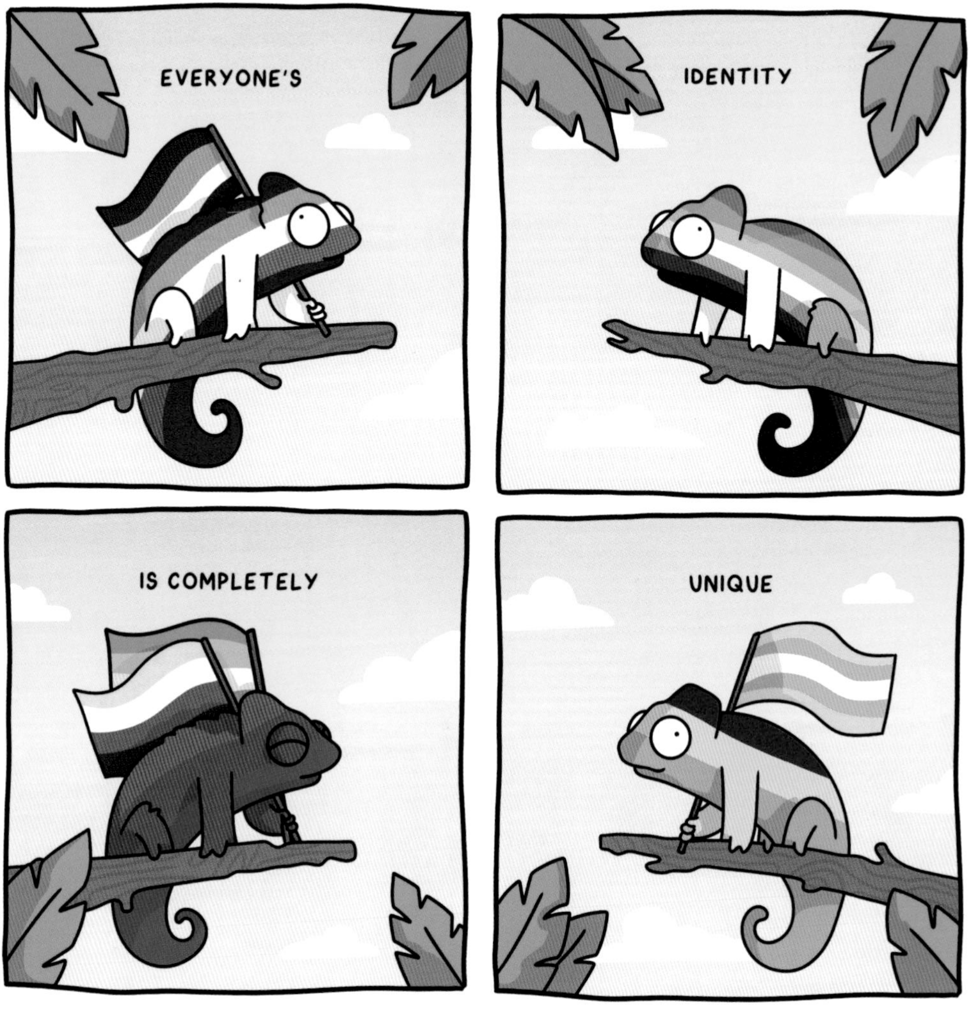
EVERYONE'S
IDENTITY
IS COMPLETELY
UNIQUE

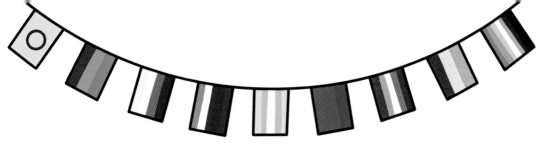

What do all these stripes mean?! In 1978, artist Gilbert Baker, an openly gay man and drag queen, designed the first rainbow flag. It was used as a way of proclaiming visibility. While it has been updated over the years, the rainbow flag remains an international symbol of LGBTQ+ pride.

Flags have since become a way to distinguish different identities within the community. This book contains a selection but there are many, many more. As they are designed by the community, new ones are created all the time. If you can't see your flag represented here it doesn't make it any less valid.

In this chapter I've included a short definition of each flag's current label. Please keep in mind that being community led, these can morph over time. Whether due to a shift in understanding or to adapt language to be more inclusive, labels definitions are ever changing and fluid. They're also open to individual interpretation and usage. Some people may define themselves differently to how their label is described here – and that is completely fine!

Importantly, everyone's experience with labels is different. Some use them, some use more than one, while others prefer to have no label at all. That is the beauty of personal identity – it is how you see yourself.

ABROSEXUAL

Fluid sexual and/or romantic orientation that changes over time. May use different terms to describe themselves over the course of their life.

ACE, ACESPEC (Asexual)

Umbrella term describing people who experience little-to-no or varying sexual attraction. May or may not experience romantic attraction. May also use terms such as gay, bi, lesbian, straight and queer to describe the direction of their romantic or sexual attraction.

AGENDER (Genderless)

Doesn't identify with any gender: not male or female, not both or either. Also described as feeling gender neutral, the absence of a feeling of gender or lacking gender, rejecting the concept of gender or feeling the concept of gender is personally irrelevant.

ARO, AROSPEC (Aromantic)

Umbrella term describing people who experience little-to-no or varying romantic attraction. May or may not experience sexual attraction. May also use terms such as gay, bi, lesbian, straight and queer to describe the direction of their romantic or sexual attraction.

AROACE (Aromantic Asexual)

Rarely or never experience either romantic or sexual attraction, making them both aromantic and asexual.

BI (Bisexual)

Umbrella term describing romantic and/or sexual orientation towards more than one gender. May also use more specific descriptions including pansexual, omnisexual, polysexual and queer.

DEMIGENDER

Nonbinary gender identities that partially identify with a particular gender, irrespective of sex assigned at birth. May identify as another gender in combination with demigender identity.

DEMIROMANTIC

Belonging to the aro spectrum, demiromantics rarely experience romantic attraction and if so, it is secondary to forming a deep emotional bond. May also use terms such as gay, bi, lesbian, straight and queer to explain the direction of their attraction.

DEMISEXUAL

Belonging to the ace spectrum, demisexuals rarely experience sexual attraction and if so, it is secondary to forming a deep emotional bond. May also use terms such as gay, bi, lesbian, straight and queer to explain the direction of their attraction.

GAY

Describes same-sex attraction (either men or women) though historically used to describe men who have romantic and/or sexual orientation towards men. Some nonbinary people also use this term.

GENDERFLUID

Describes a gender identity and/or expression that changes over time.

GENDERQUEER

Umbrella term for people whose gender identity doesn't follow binary gender norms. May be nonbinary, agender, genderfluid or another gender identity.

INTERSEX

Born with genetic, hormonal or physical sex characteristics that don't fit medical/societal assumed norms for male or female bodies. May identify as male, female, nonbinary or other gender identities. May or may not identify as part of the LGBTQ+ community.

LESBIAN

Women who have a romantic and/or sexual orientation towards women. Some lesbians prefer to identify as gay or as gay women. Some nonbinary people also use this term.

NONBINARY

Umbrella term for people whose gender identity doesn't sit comfortably with 'male' or 'female', including those who align with some aspects of binary identities and others who reject them entirely.

OMNI (Omnisexual)

Sexual attraction to people of all sexes and gender identities where gender has an influence on one's attraction, though doesn't necessarily mean that certain genders are preferred.

PAN (Pansexual)

Romantic and/or sexual attraction towards others, regardless of sex or gender.

POLYAMOROUS

Romantically or sexually involved with more than one person at the same time, where each person in the relationship is aware of and consents to its non-monogamous nature. Applicable to both LGBTQ+ and heterosexual relationships.

POLYSEXUAL

Sexual attraction to various genders including at least two and up to many. Attraction may be preferenced by gender but this is not always the case.

QUEER

Broad identifier for individuals and/or the community of people not cisgender and/or heterosexual. Can be used instead of or in addition to other sexual identifiers such as lesbian, bisexual or gay. Can also refer to gender identity or gender expression, either as a standalone term or part of another, like genderqueer. As a reclaimed word, queer has been used to demonstrate inclusivity and fight for LGBTQ+ rights. Like all labels, its use is personal and unique.

TRANS (Transgender)

Gender identity differs from sex assigned at birth.
May also use the terms: trans man, trans woman,
transmasculine and transfeminine. Other labels include:
genderqueer, genderfluid, nonbinary, genderless,
agender and nongender, among others.

TWO-SPIRIT

Used by some Indigenous cultures to describe
traditional cultural understandings of gender and
sexuality outside Western binaries. As these traditions
are culturally and spiritually specific, two-spirit cannot
be claimed or used by people not from this heritage.

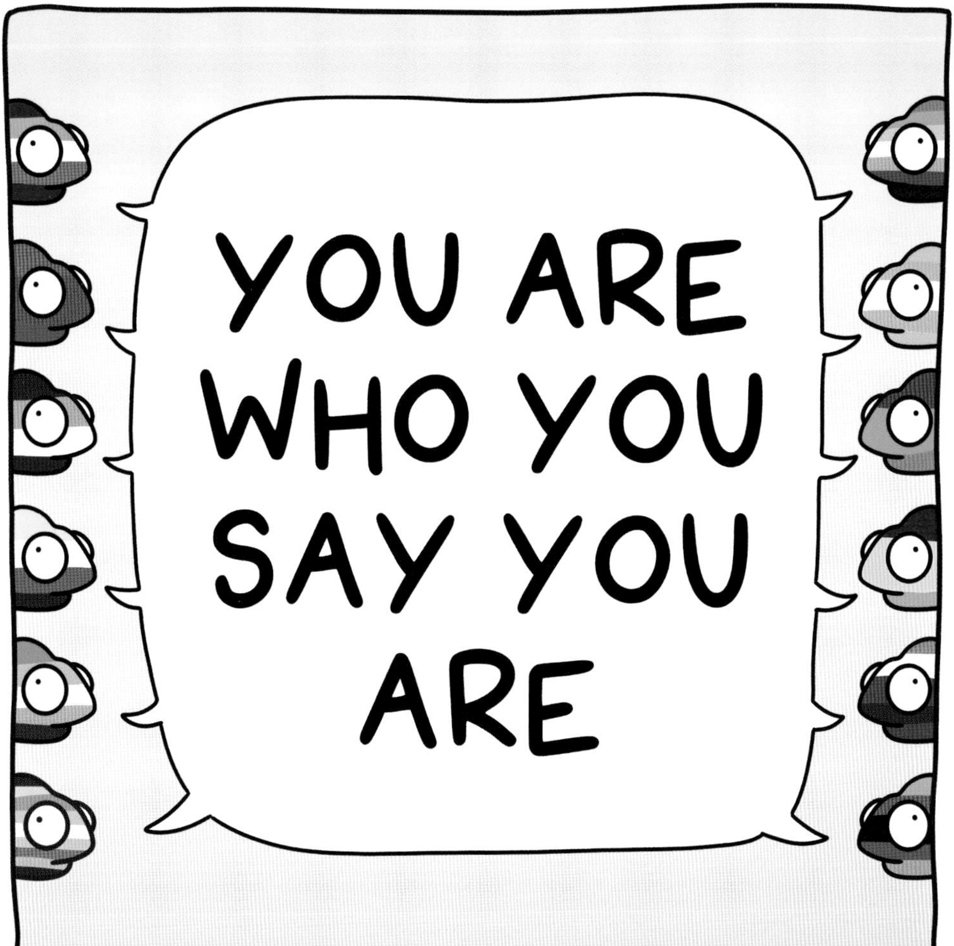
YOU ARE WHO YOU SAY YOU ARE

CHAPTER 2

COMING OUT

A light-hearted look at the trials and
tribulations of coming out (or choosing not to)

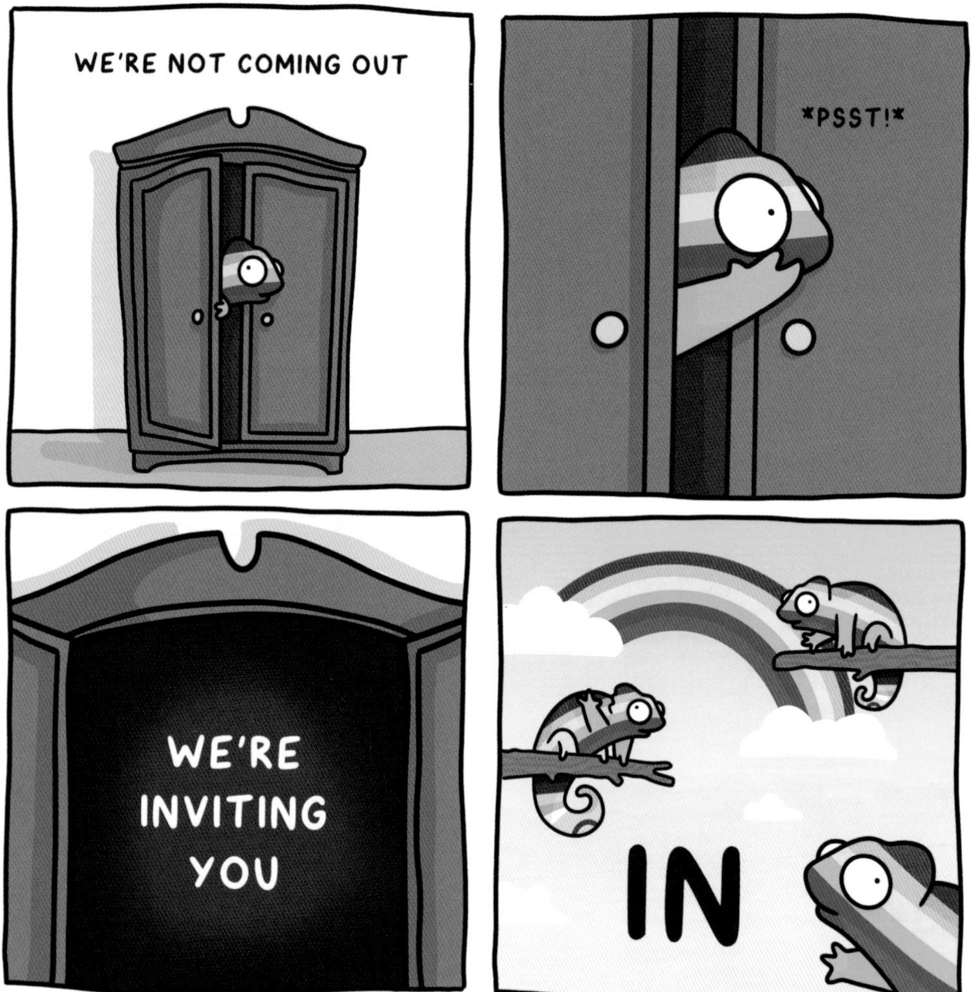
WE'RE NOT COMING OUT
PSST!
WE'RE INVITING YOU
IN

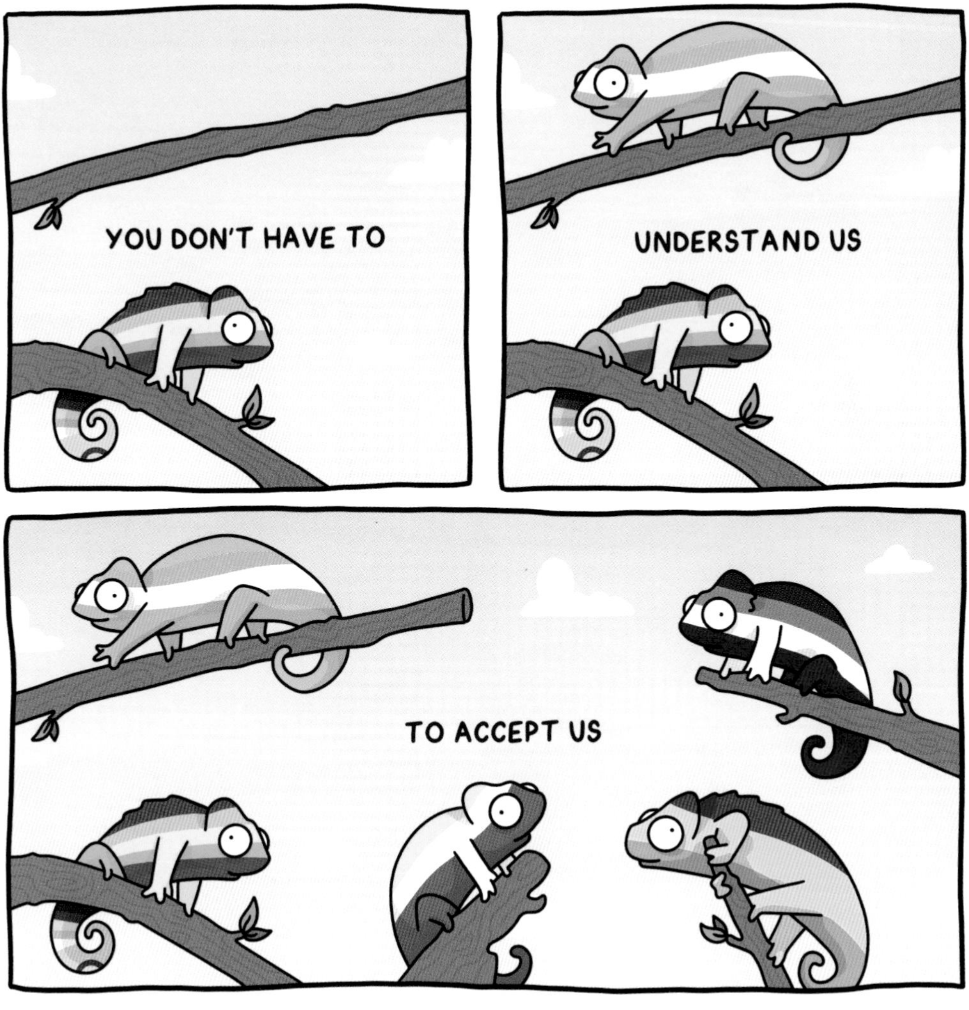
YOU DON'T HAVE TO
UNDERSTAND US
TO ACCEPT US

YOU'RE NEVER
TOO OLD
OR TOO YOUNG

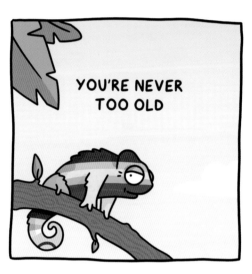

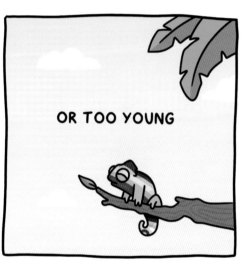

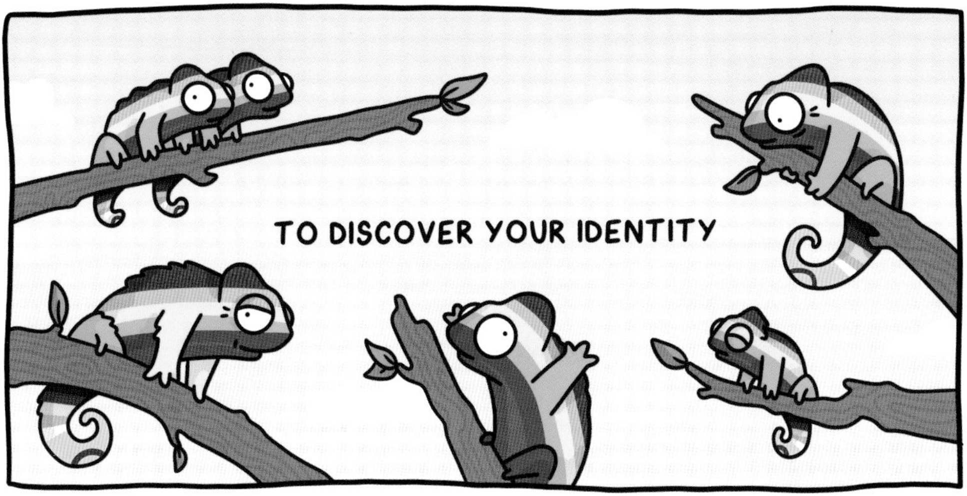
TO DISCOVER YOUR IDENTITY

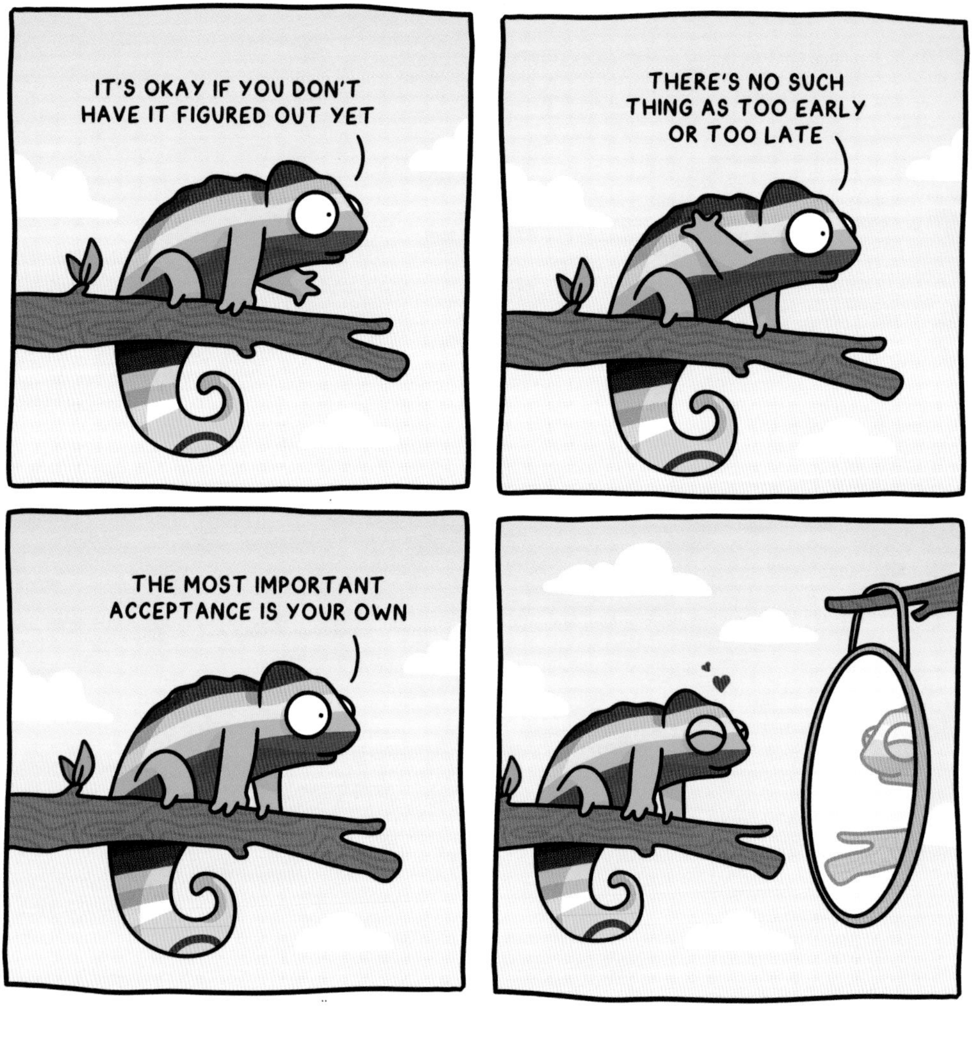
IT'S OKAY IF YOU DON'T HAVE IT FIGURED OUT YET
THERE'S NO SUCH THING AS TOO EARLY OR TOO LATE
THE MOST IMPORTANT ACCEPTANCE IS YOUR OWN

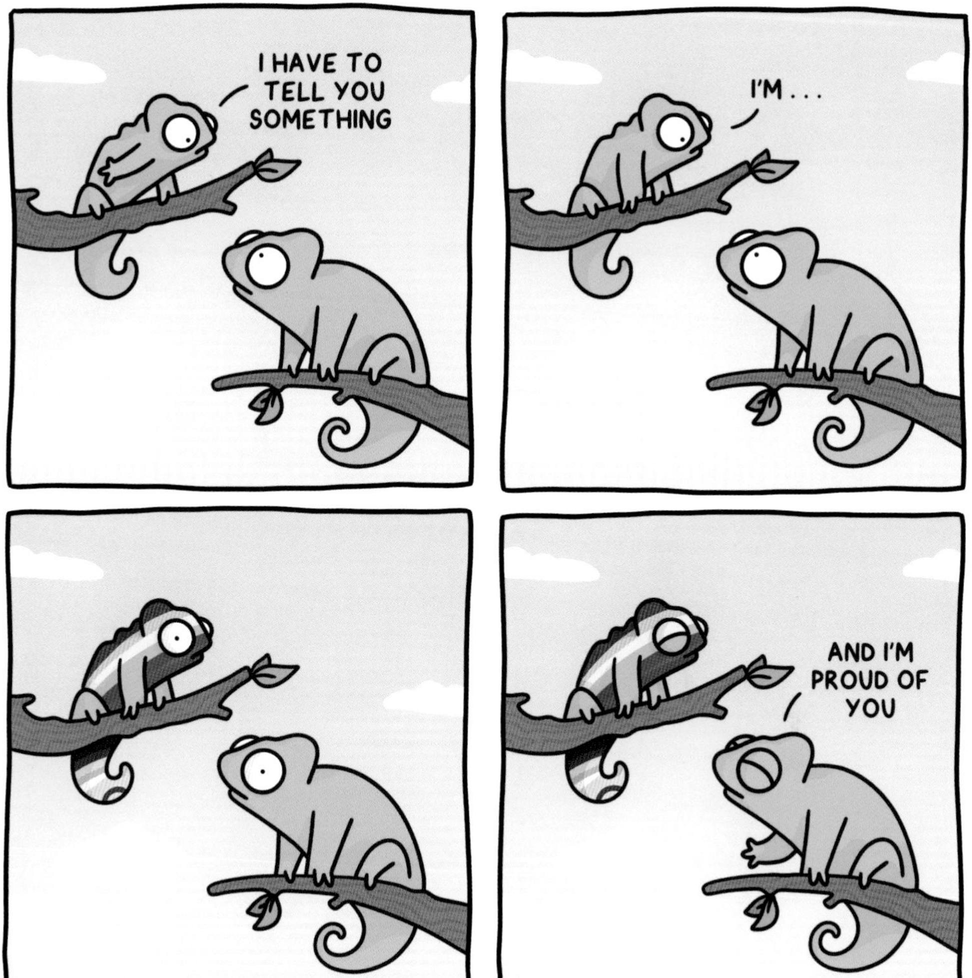
I HAVE TO TELL YOU SOMETHING
I'M . . .
AND I'M PROUD OF YOU

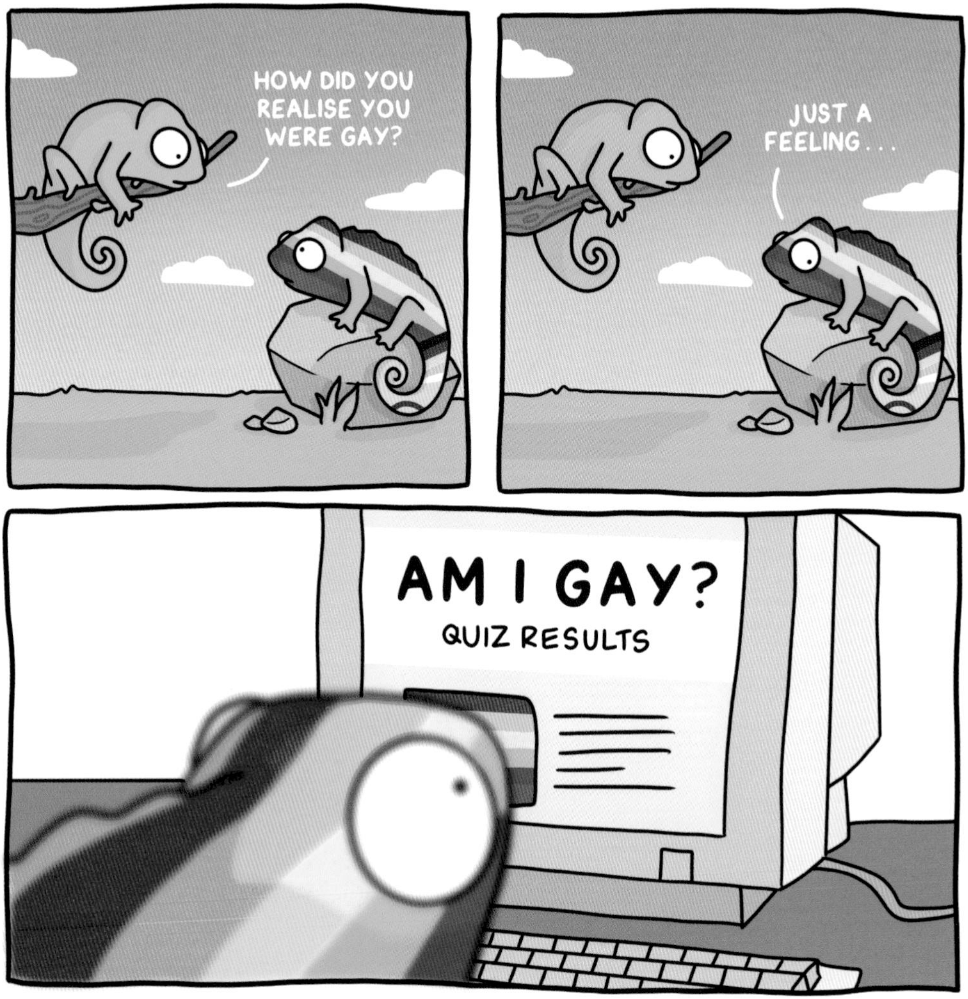
HOW DID YOU REALISE YOU WERE GAY?
JUST A FEELING . . .
AM I GAY?
QUIZ RESULTS

IDENTITY

CAN

BE

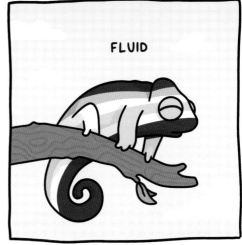

FLUID

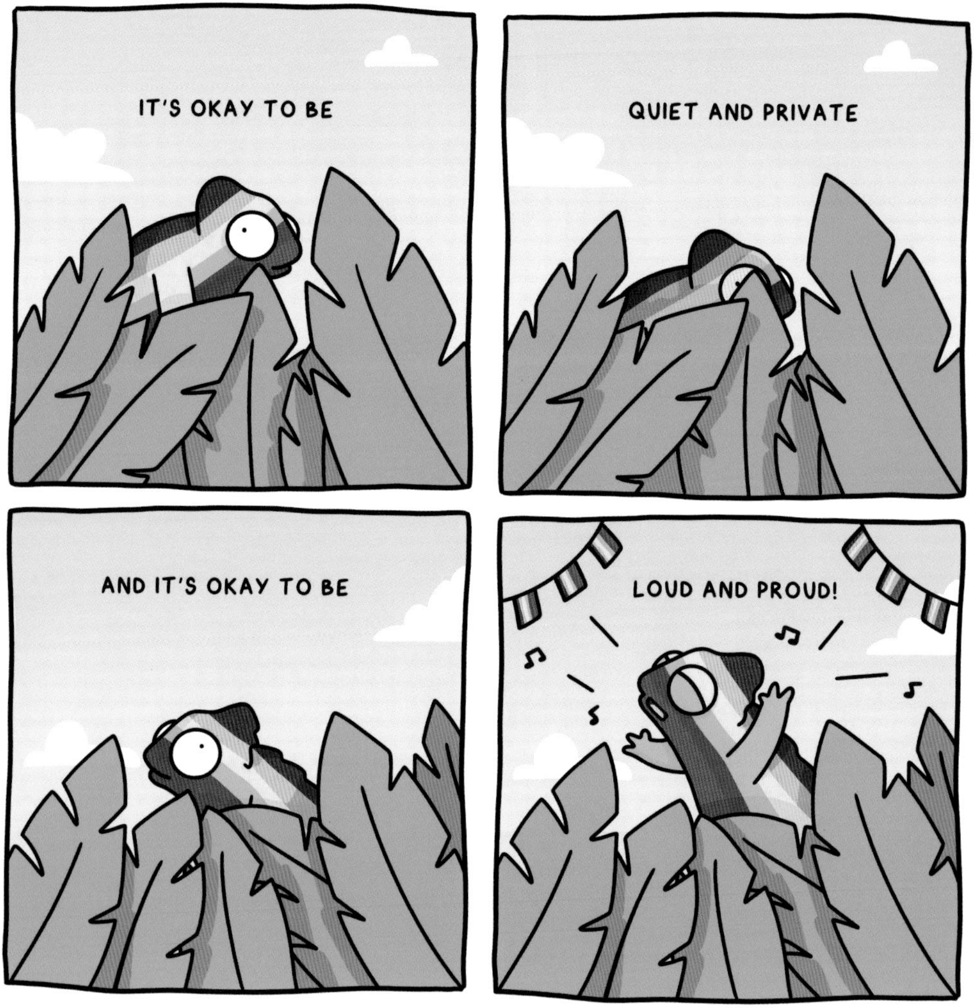
IT'S OKAY TO BE
QUIET AND PRIVATE
AND IT'S OKAY TO BE
LOUD AND PROUD!

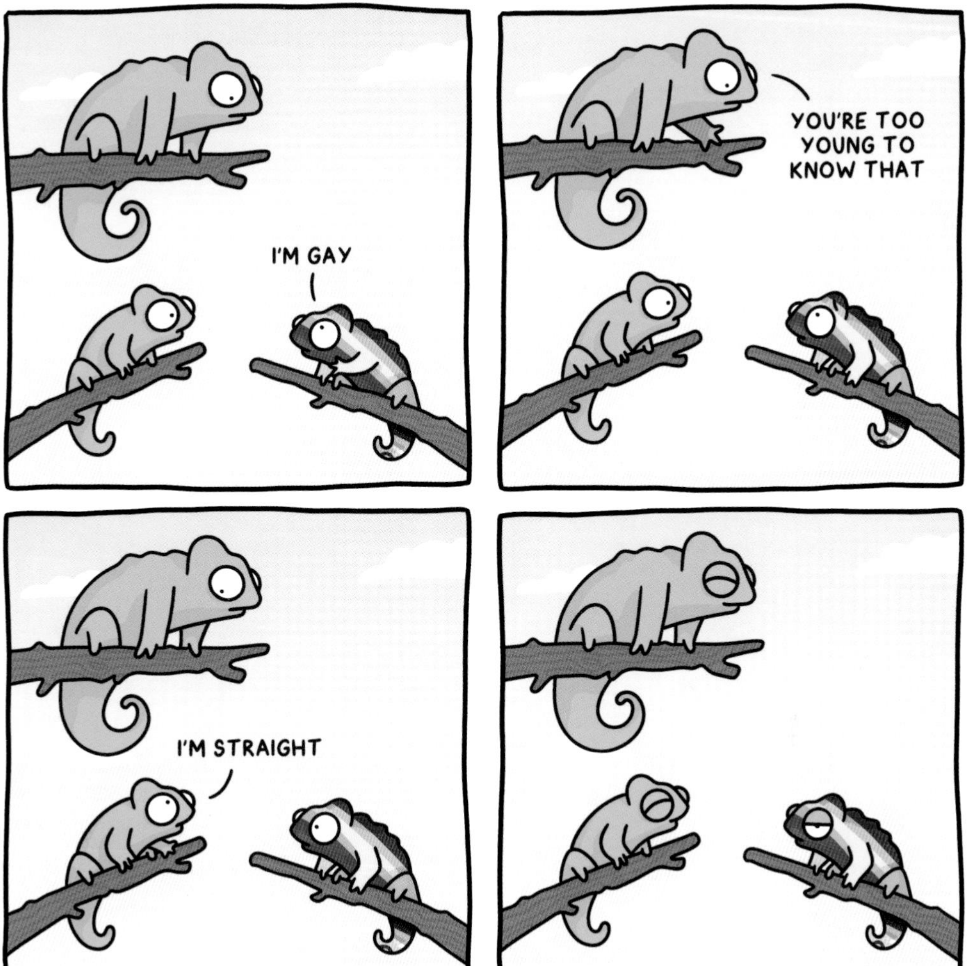
I'M GAY
YOU'RE TOO YOUNG TO KNOW THAT
I'M STRAIGHT

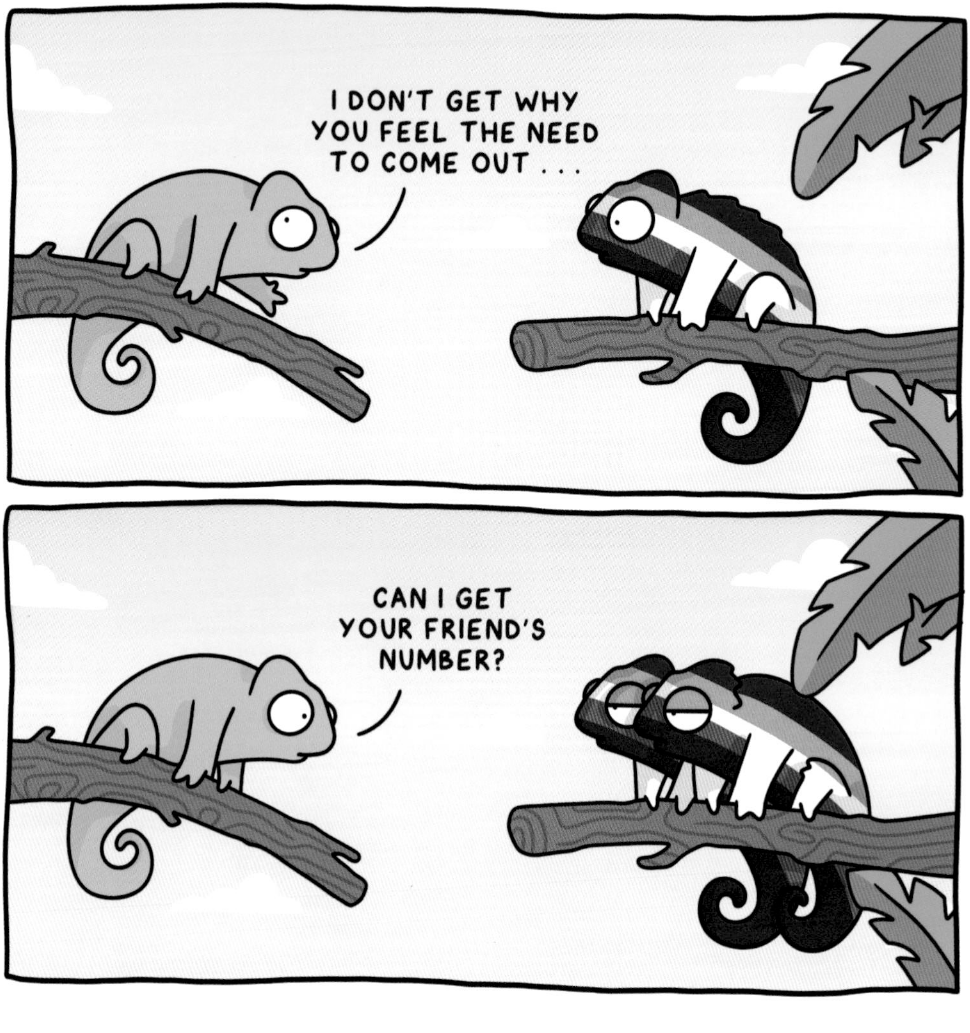
I DON'T GET WHY YOU FEEL THE NEED TO COME OUT . . .
CAN I GET YOUR FRIEND'S NUMBER?

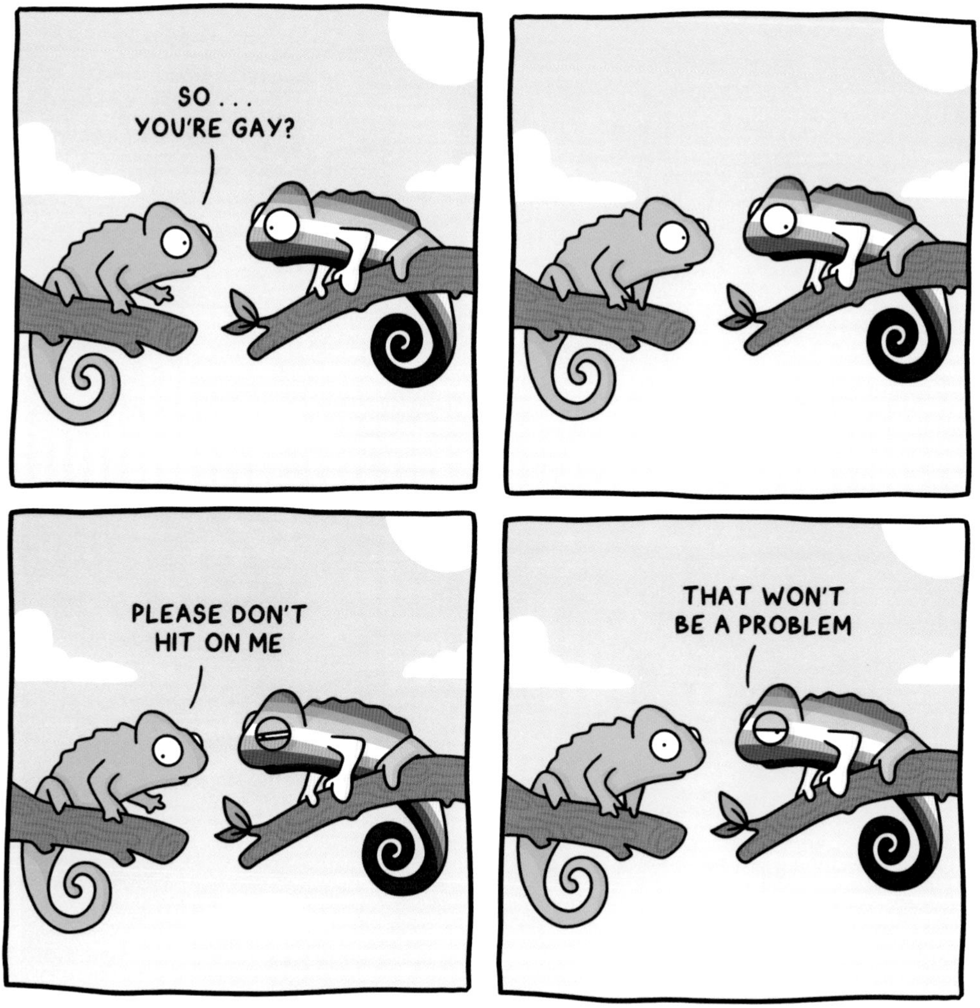
SO . . .
YOU'RE GAY?
PLEASE DON'T
HIT ON ME
THAT WON'T
BE A PROBLEM

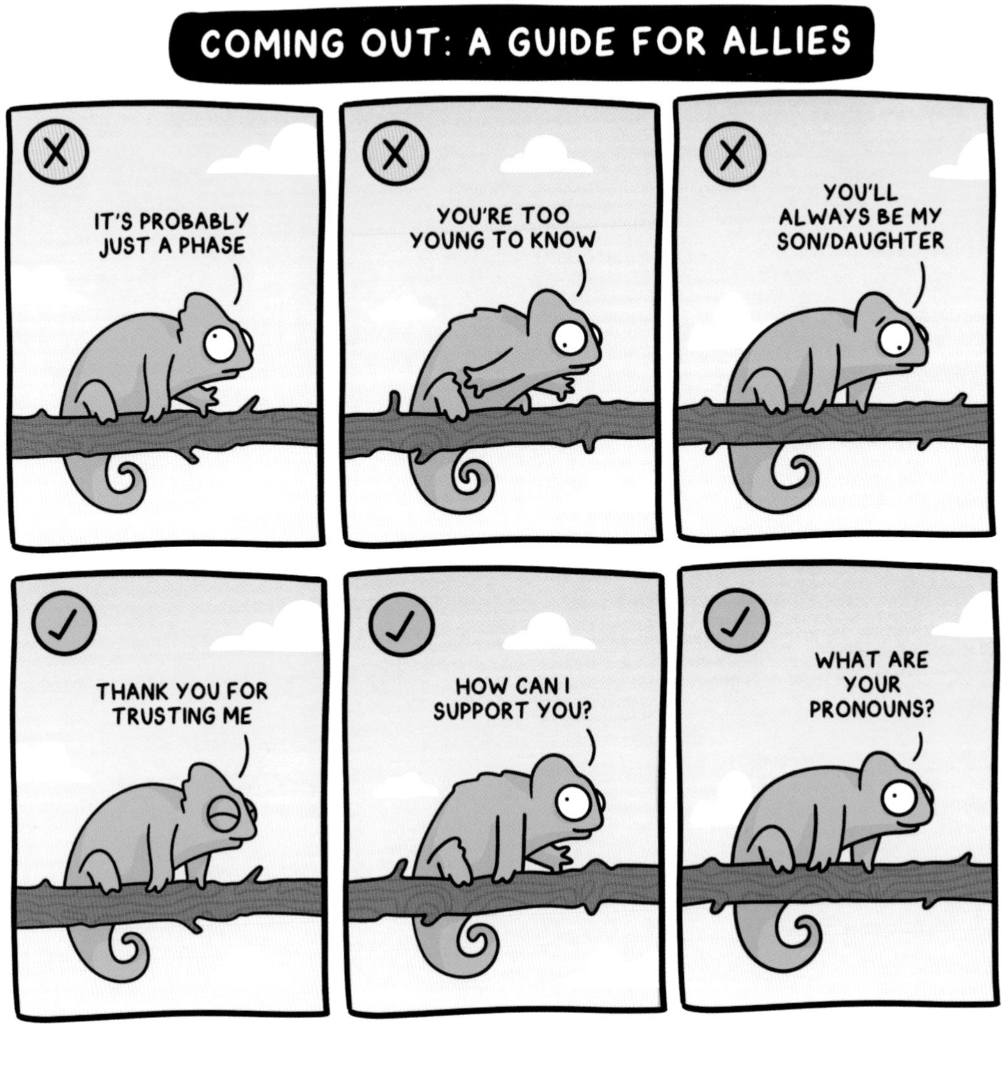
COMING OUT: A GUIDE FOR ALLIES
IT'S PROBABLY JUST A PHASE
YOU'RE TOO YOUNG TO KNOW
YOU'LL ALWAYS BE MY SON/DAUGHTER
THANK YOU FOR TRUSTING ME
HOW CAN I SUPPORT YOU?
WHAT ARE YOUR PRONOUNS?

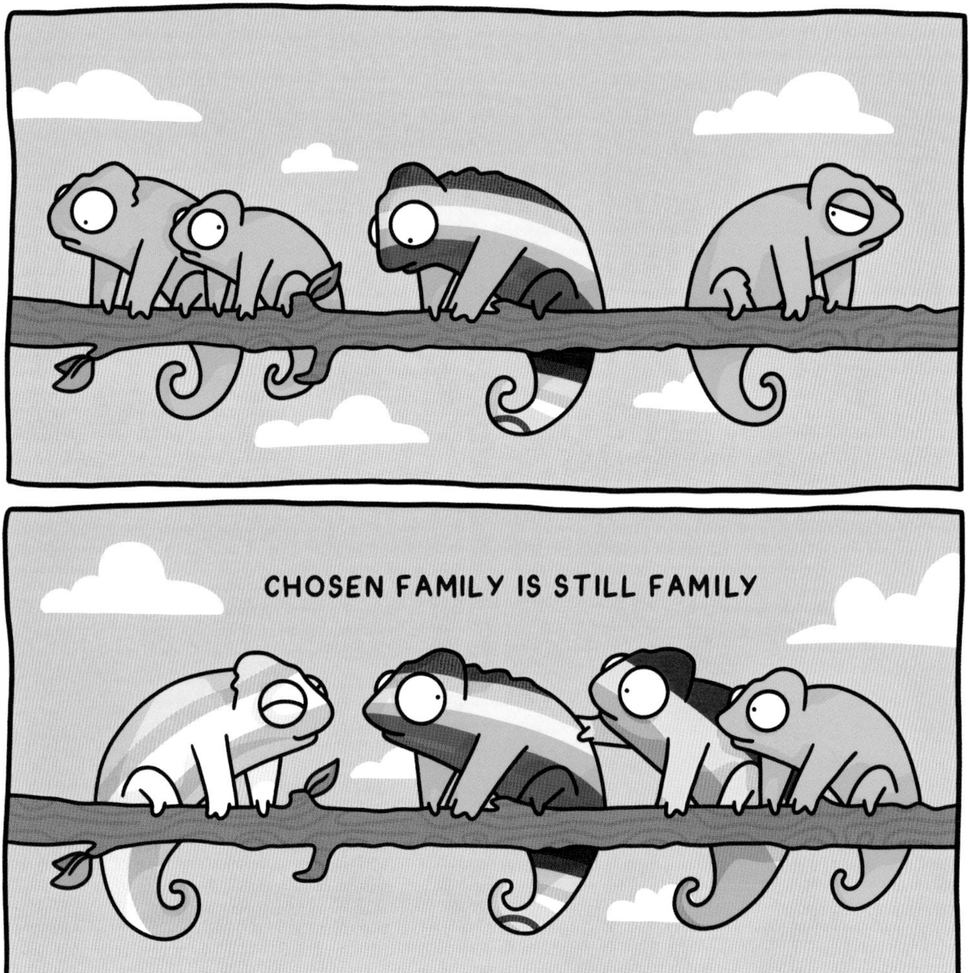
CHOSEN FAMILY IS STILL FAMILY

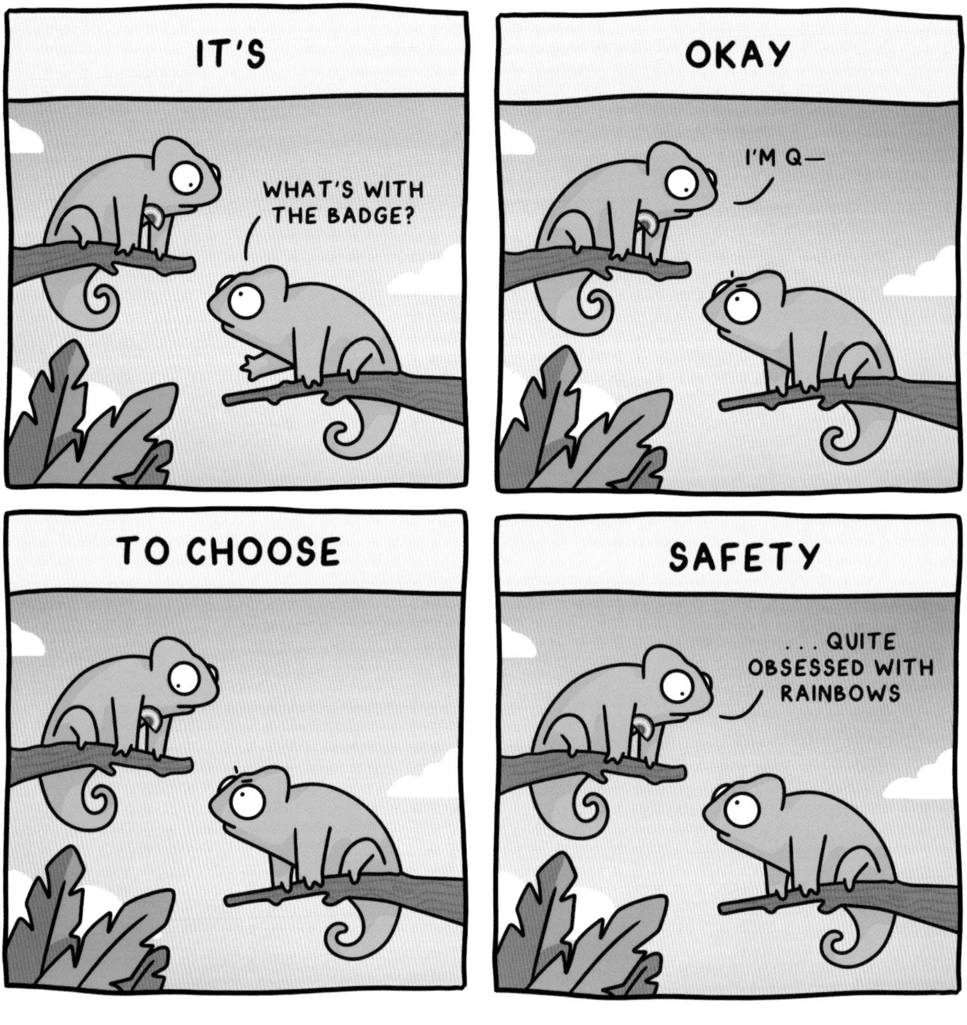
IT'S
WHAT'S WITH THE BADGE?
OKAY
I'M Q—
TO CHOOSE
SAFETY
. . . QUITE OBSESSED WITH RAINBOWS

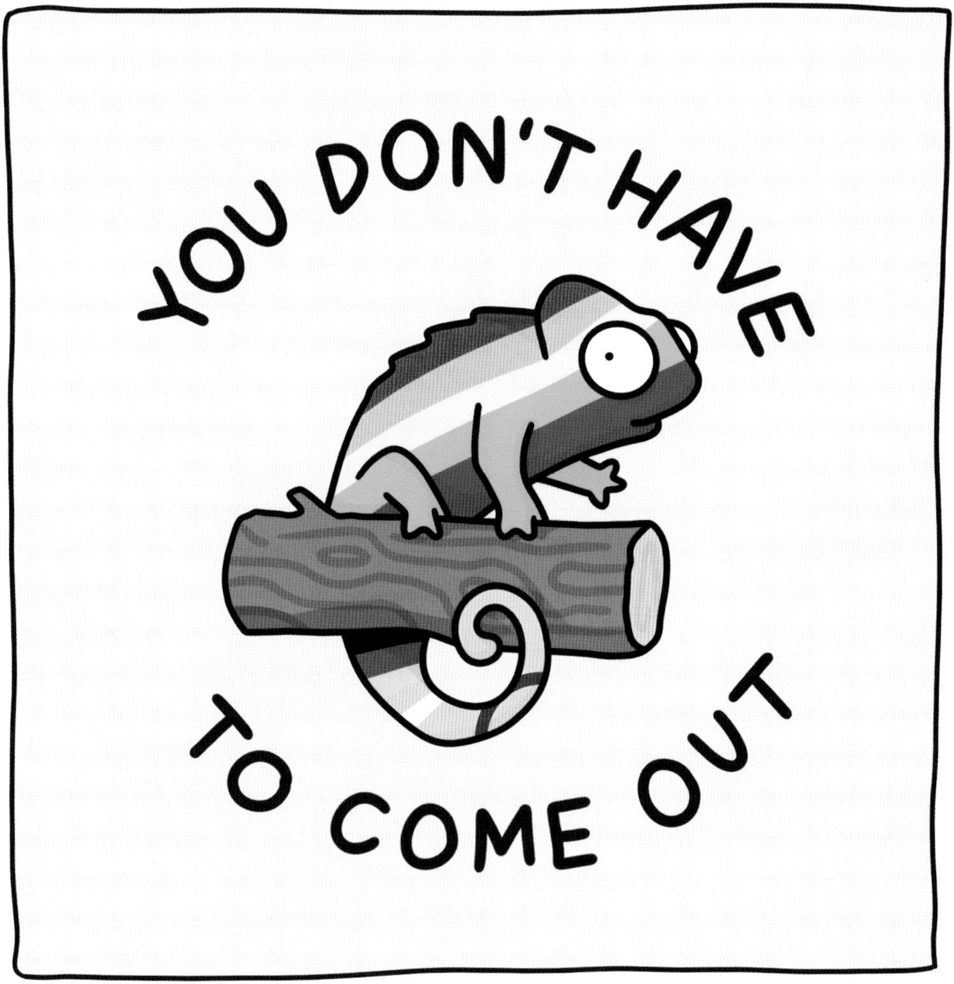
YOU DON'T HAVE
TO COME OUT

CHAPTER 3

PLEASE STOP

Some of the infuriating, frustrating
and downright bizarre things we've heard

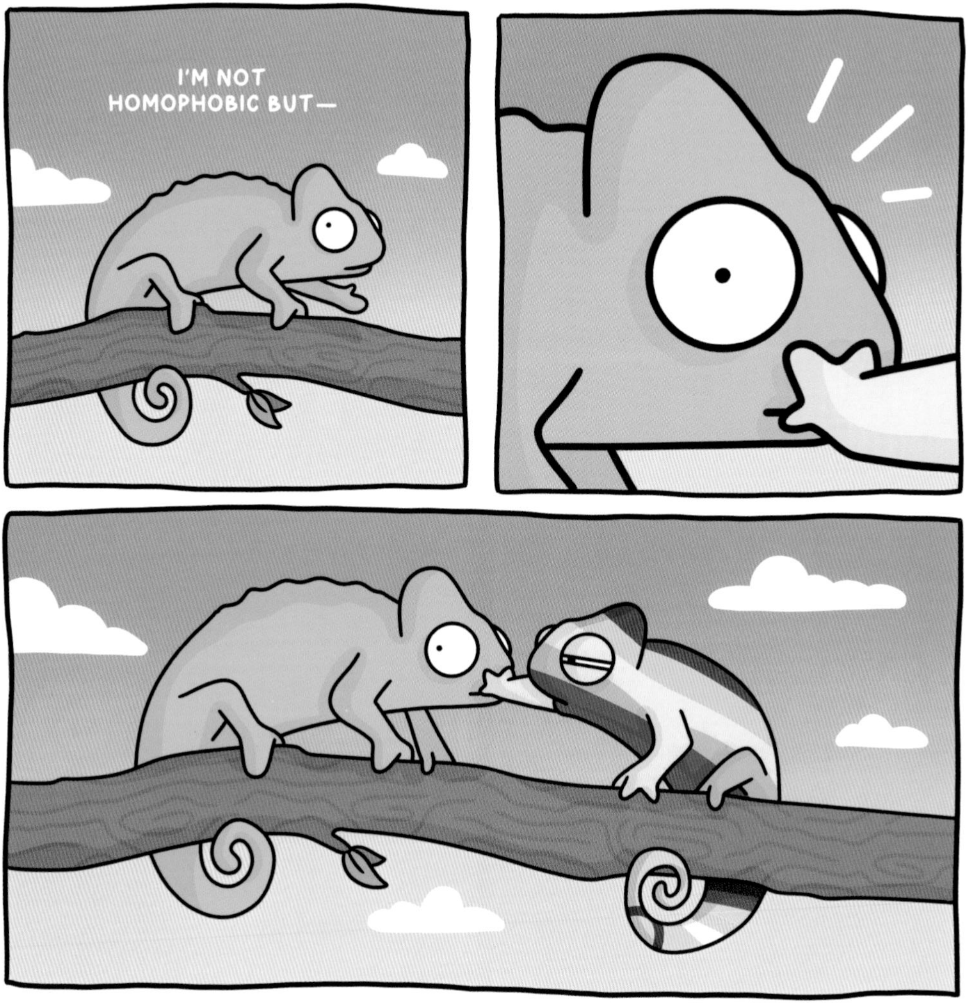
I'M NOT
HOMOPHOBIC BUT—

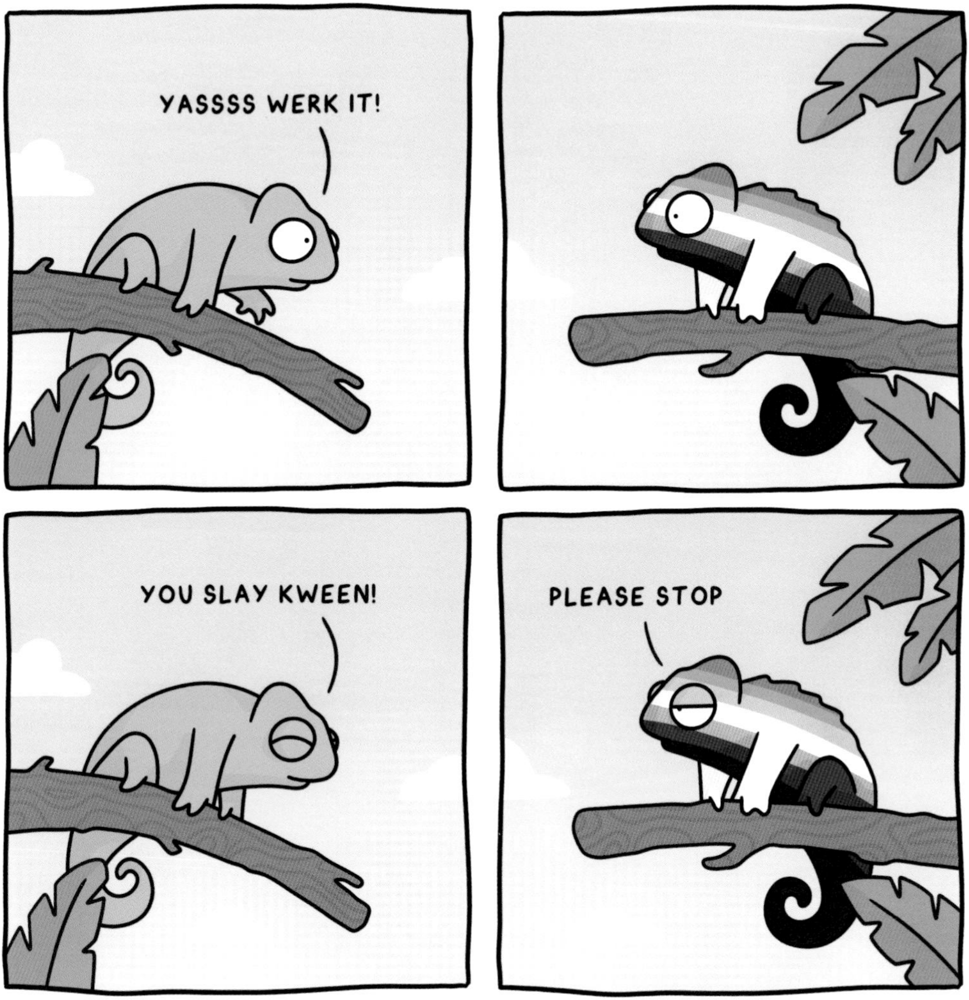
YASSSS WERK IT!
YOU SLAY KWEEN!
PLEASE STOP

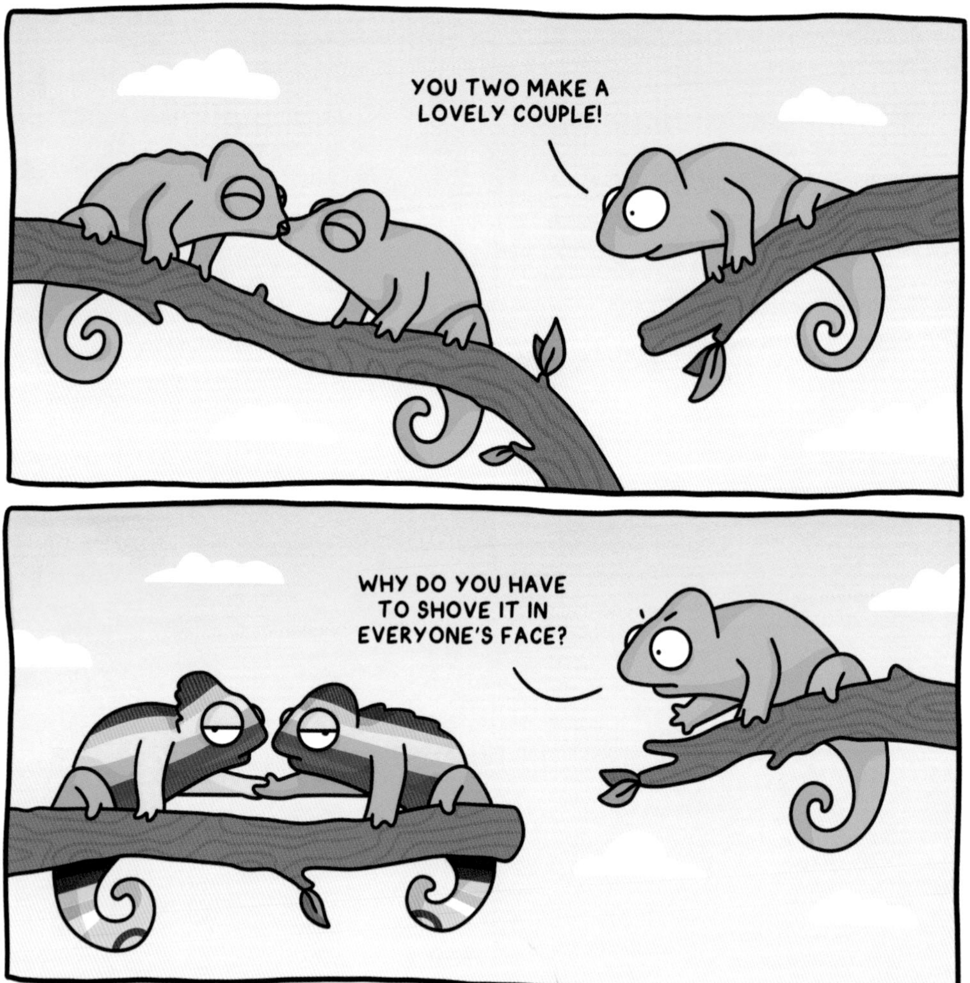
YOU TWO MAKE A LOVELY COUPLE!
WHY DO YOU HAVE TO SHOVE IT IN EVERYONE'S FACE?

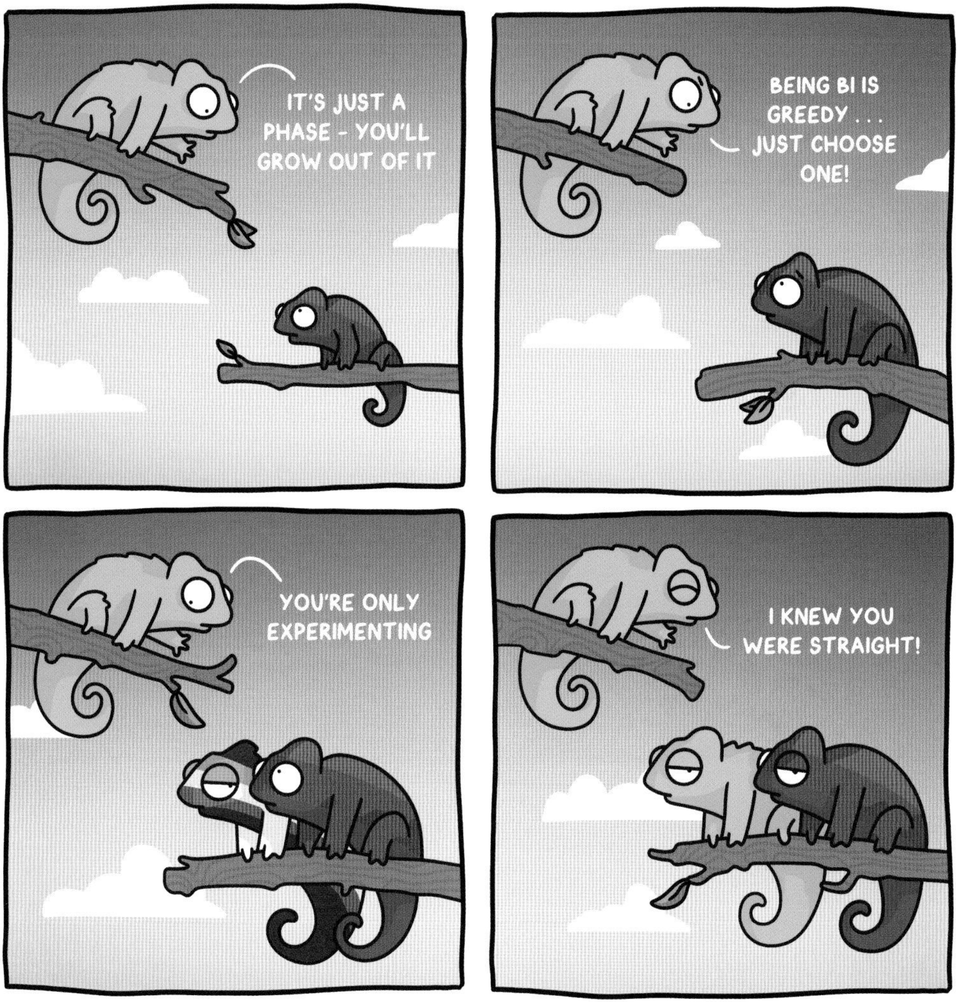
IT'S JUST A PHASE - YOU'LL GROW OUT OF IT
BEING BI IS GREEDY . . . JUST CHOOSE ONE!
YOU'RE ONLY EXPERIMENTING
I KNEW YOU WERE STRAIGHT!

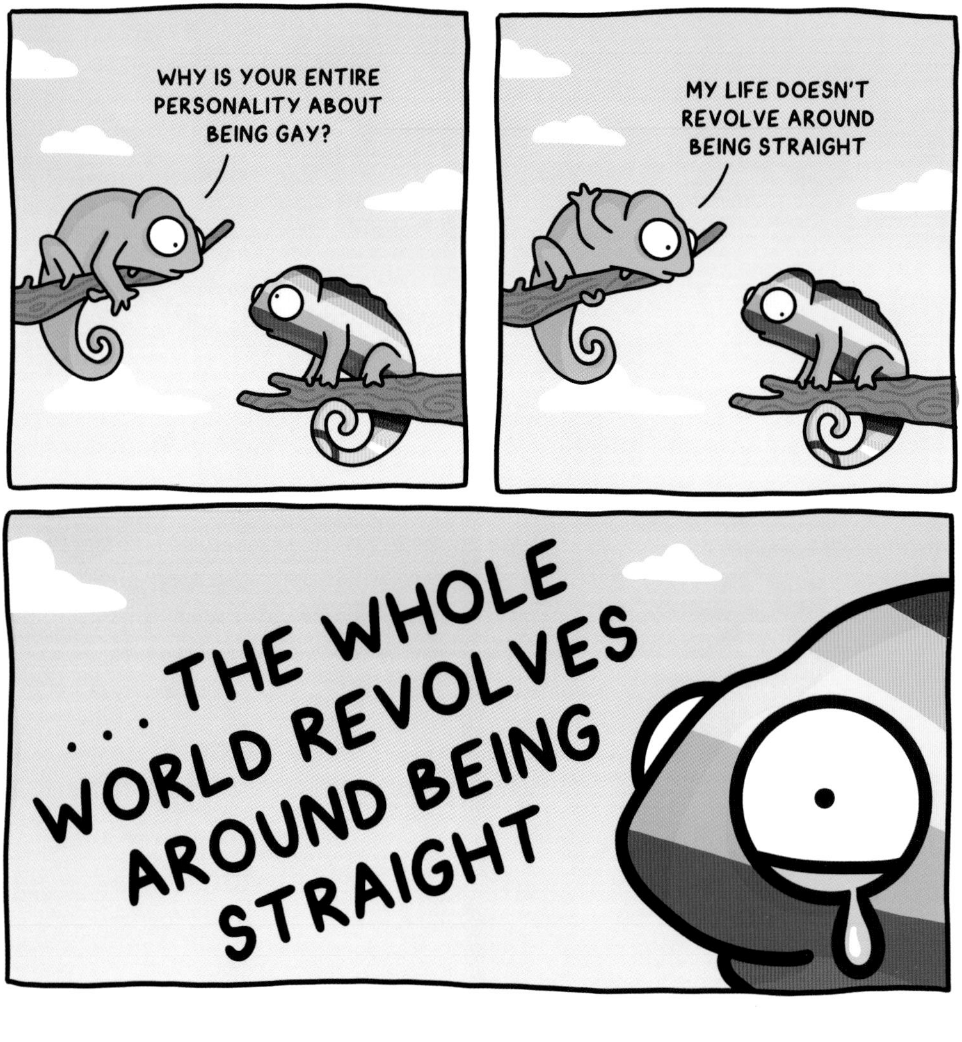
WHY IS YOUR ENTIRE PERSONALITY ABOUT BEING GAY?
MY LIFE DOESN'T REVOLVE AROUND BEING STRAIGHT
. . . THE WHOLE WORLD REVOLVES AROUND BEING STRAIGHT

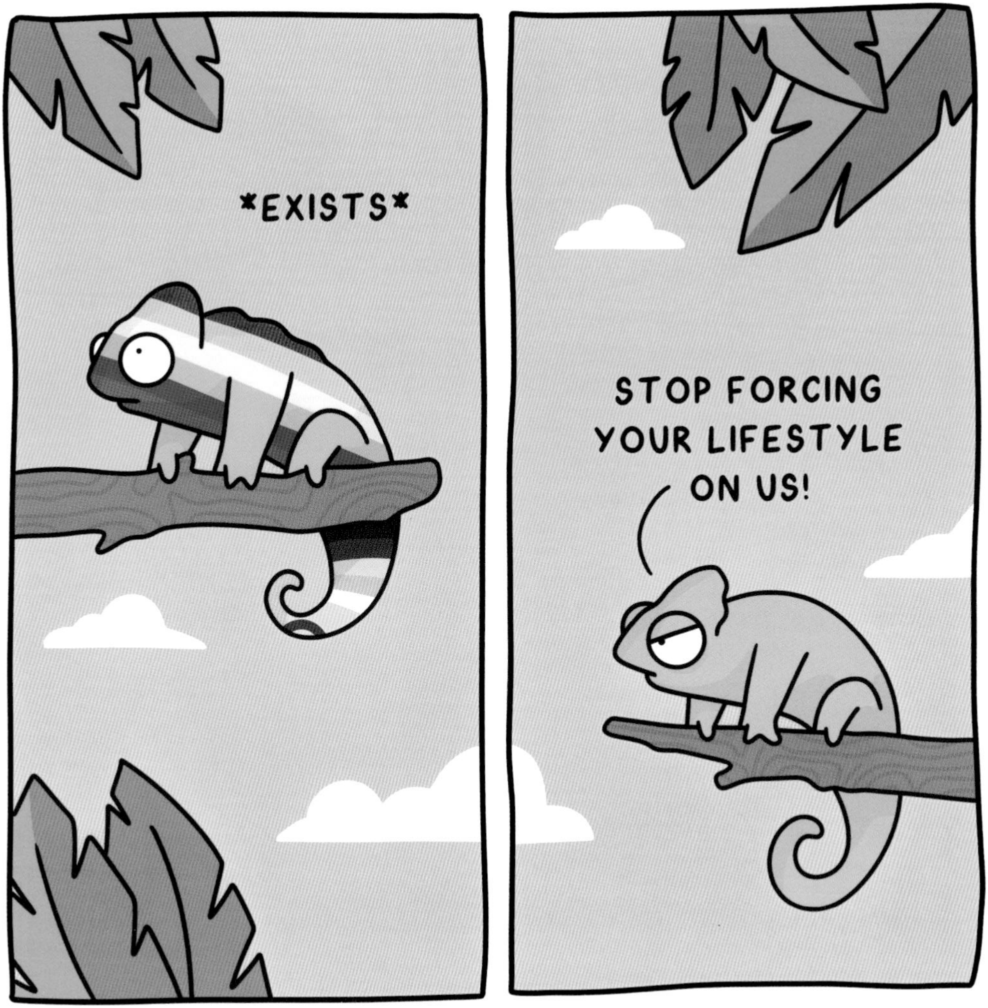
EXISTS
STOP FORCING YOUR LIFESTYLE ON US!

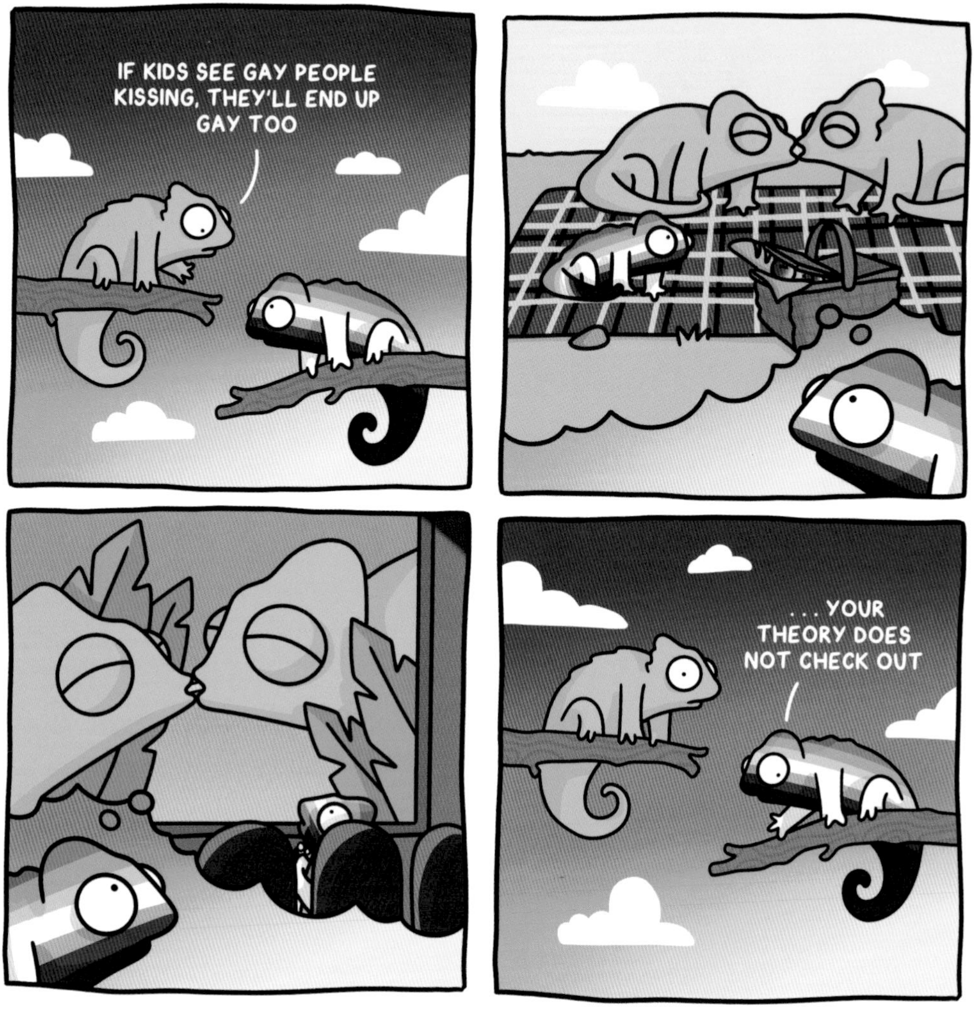
IF KIDS SEE GAY PEOPLE KISSING, THEY'LL END UP GAY TOO
. . . YOUR THEORY DOES NOT CHECK OUT

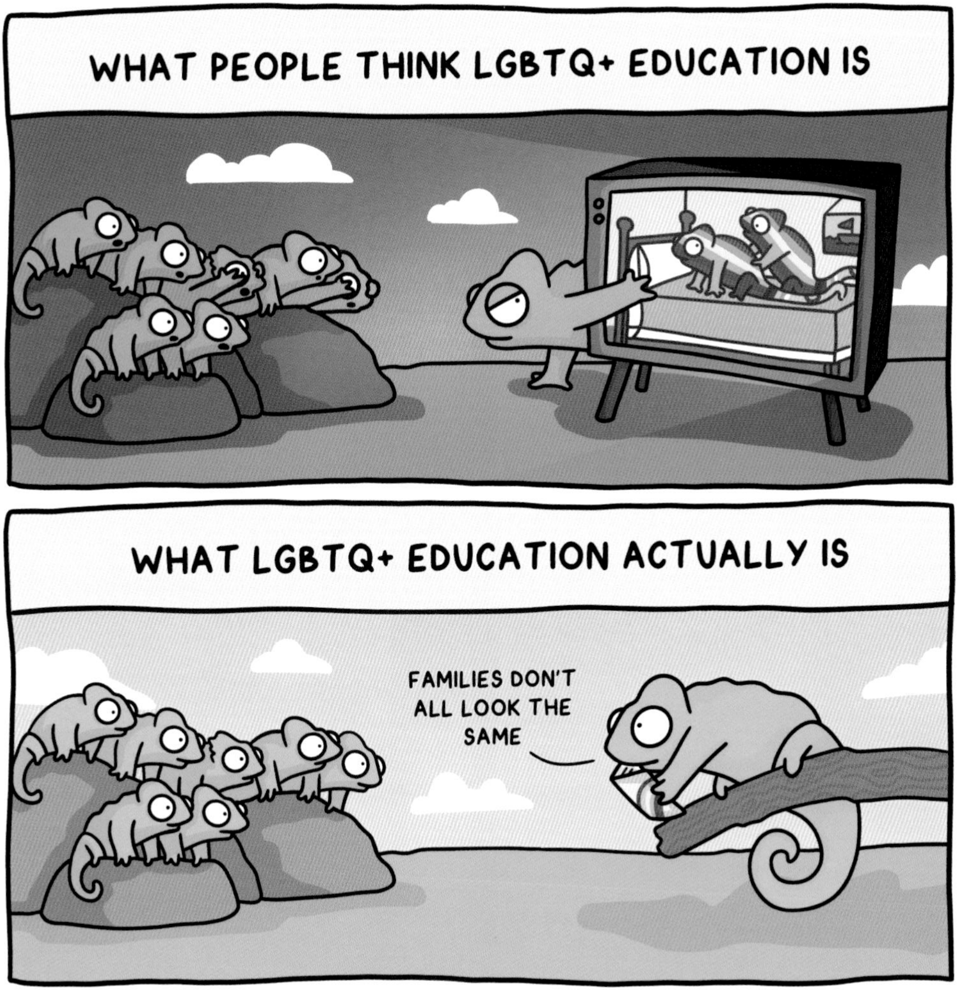
WHAT PEOPLE THINK LGBTQ+ EDUCATION IS
WHAT LGBTQ+ EDUCATION ACTUALLY IS
FAMILIES DON'T ALL LOOK THE SAME

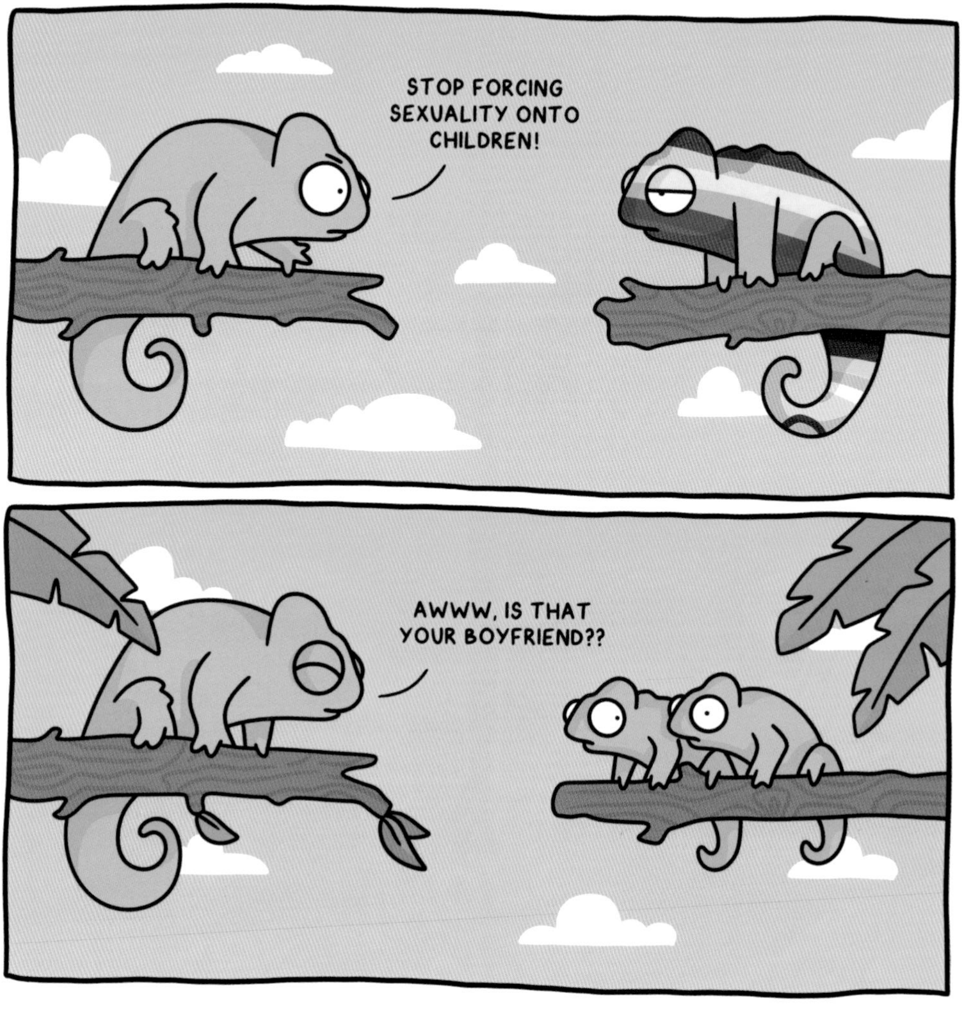
STOP FORCING SEXUALITY ONTO CHILDREN!
AWWW, IS THAT YOUR BOYFRIEND??

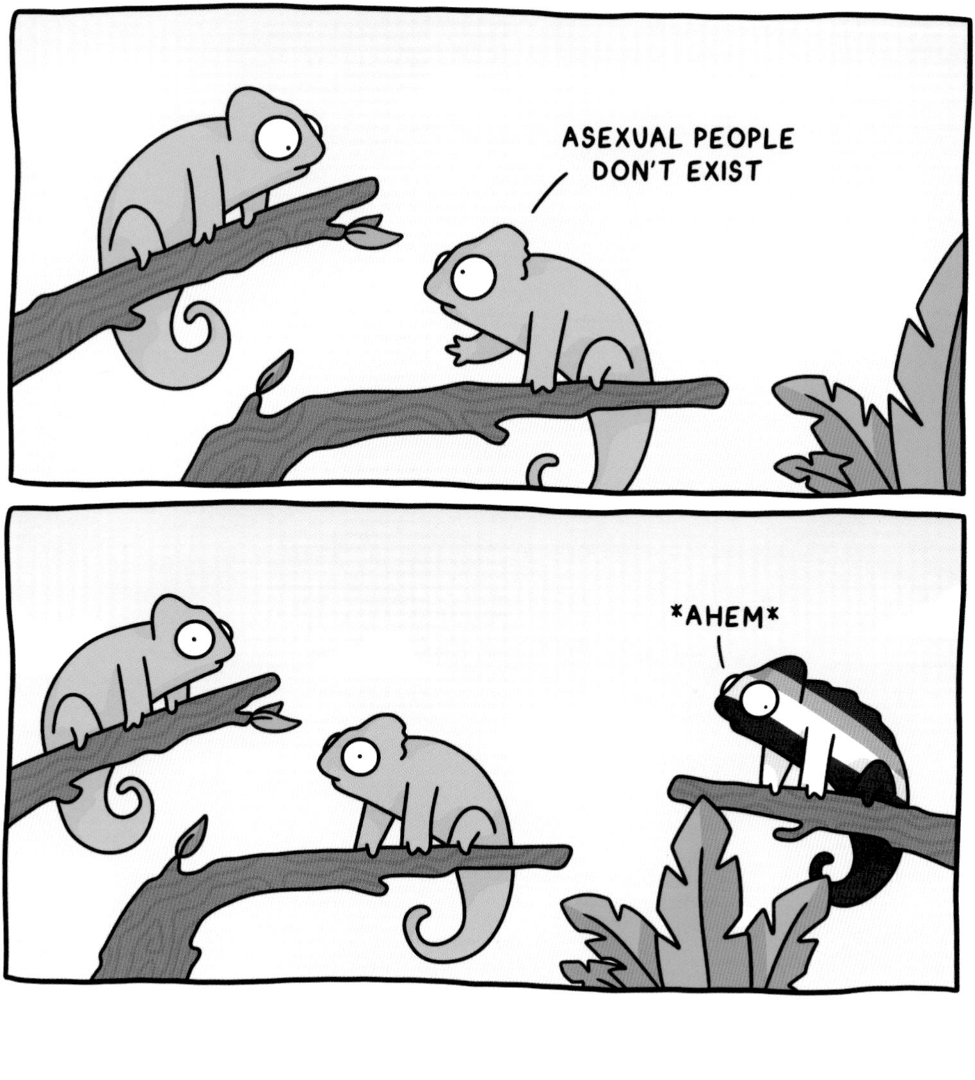
ASEXUAL PEOPLE DON'T EXIST
AHEM

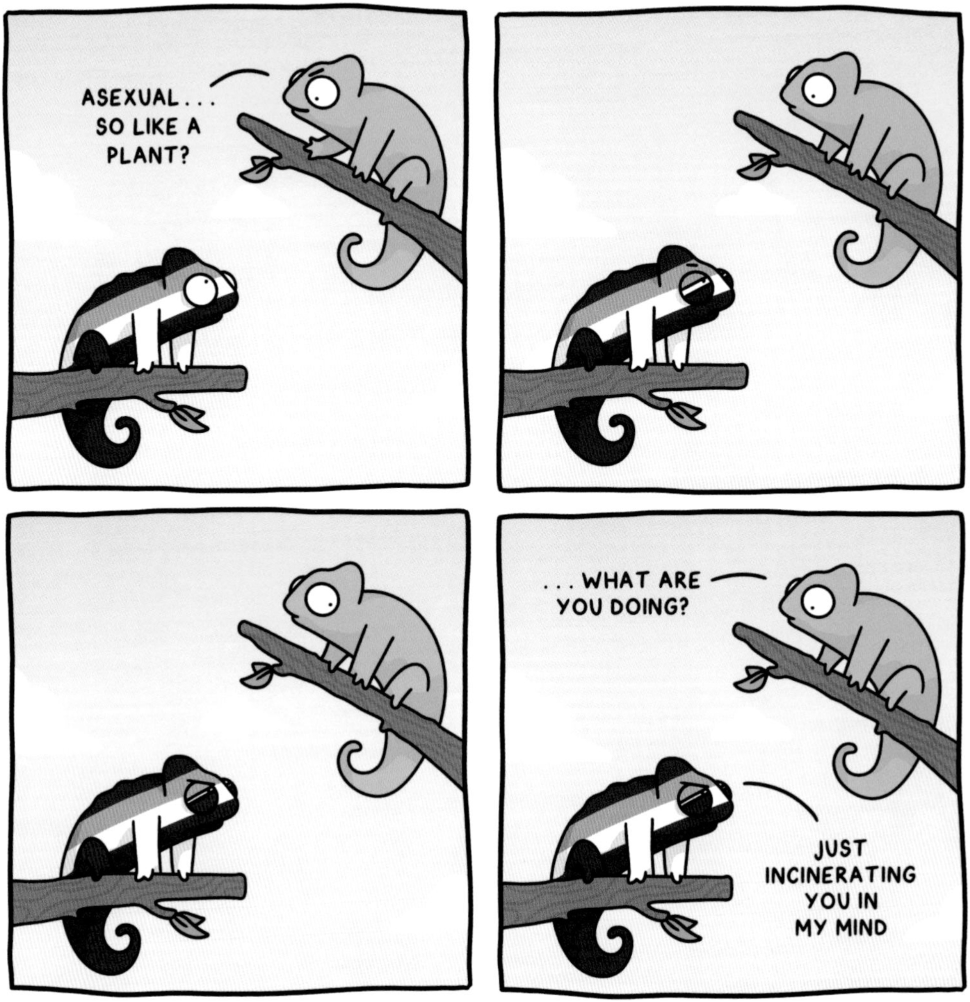
ASEXUAL...
SO LIKE A
PLANT?
...WHAT ARE
YOU DOING?
JUST
INCINERATING
YOU IN
MY MIND

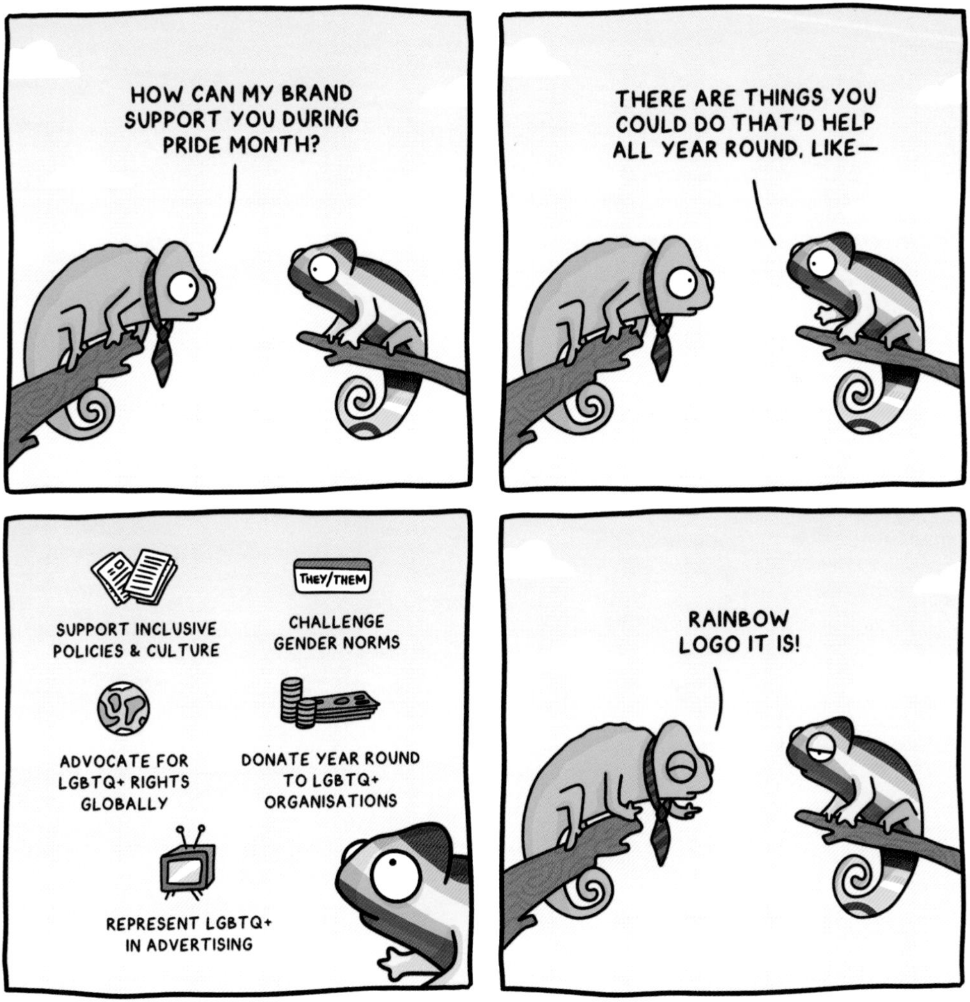
HOW CAN MY BRAND SUPPORT YOU DURING PRIDE MONTH?
THERE ARE THINGS YOU COULD DO THAT'D HELP ALL YEAR ROUND, LIKE—
THEY/THEM
SUPPORT INCLUSIVE POLICIES & CULTURE
CHALLENGE GENDER NORMS
ADVOCATE FOR LGBTQ+ RIGHTS GLOBALLY
DONATE YEAR ROUND TO LGBTQ+ ORGANISATIONS
REPRESENT LGBTQ+ IN ADVERTISING
RAINBOW LOGO IT IS!

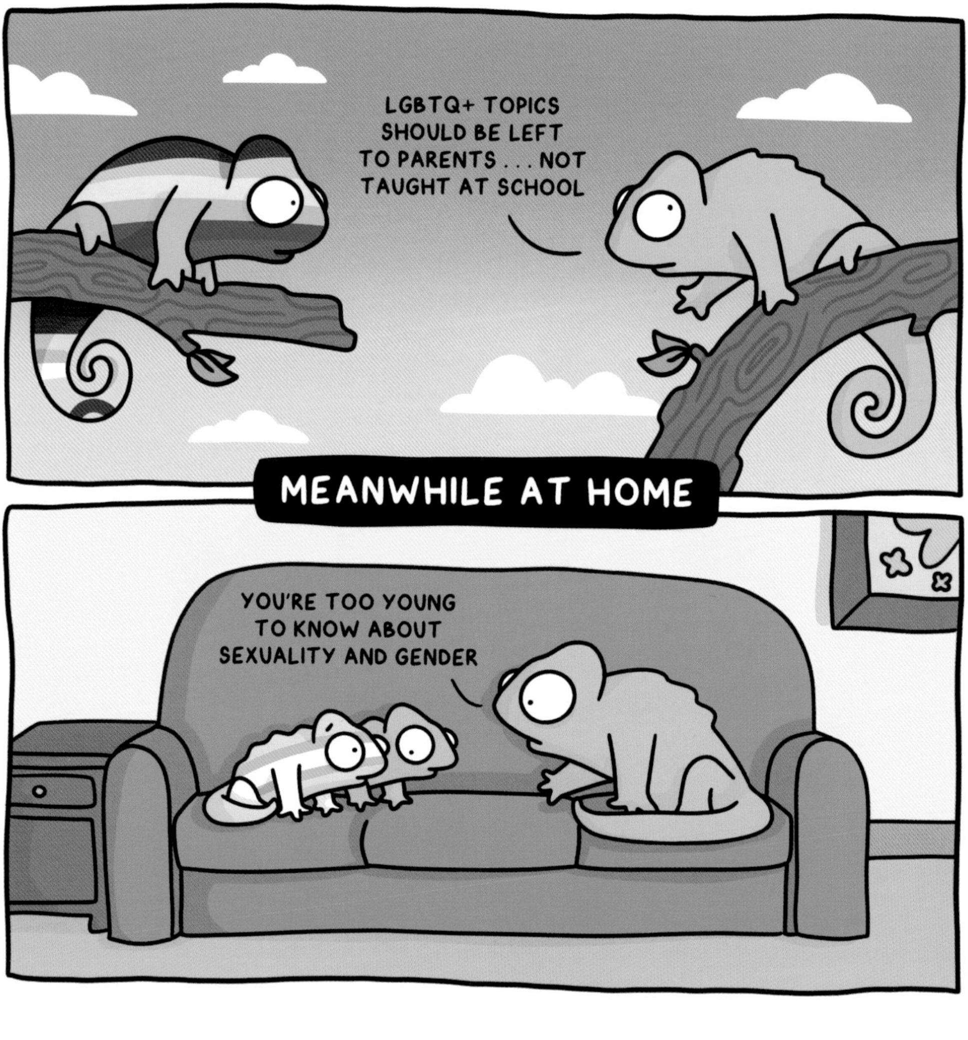
LGBTQ+ TOPICS SHOULD BE LEFT TO PARENTS . . . NOT TAUGHT AT SCHOOL
MEANWHILE AT HOME
YOU'RE TOO YOUNG TO KNOW ABOUT SEXUALITY AND GENDER

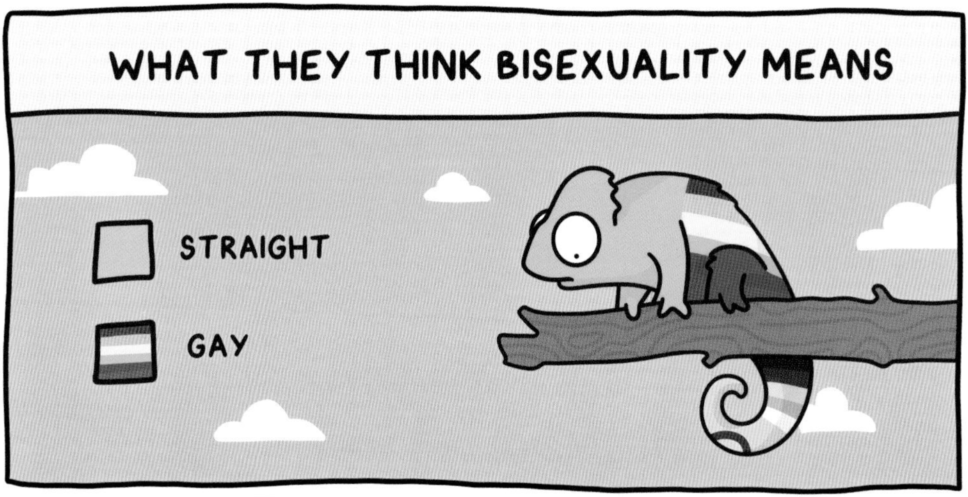
WHAT THEY THINK BISEXUALITY MEANS
STRAIGHT
GAY

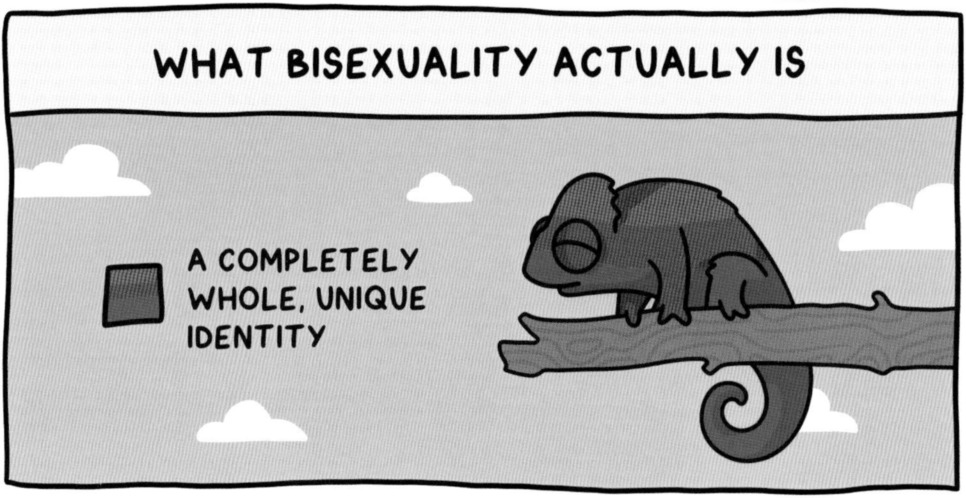
WHAT BISEXUALITY ACTUALLY IS
A COMPLETELY WHOLE, UNIQUE IDENTITY

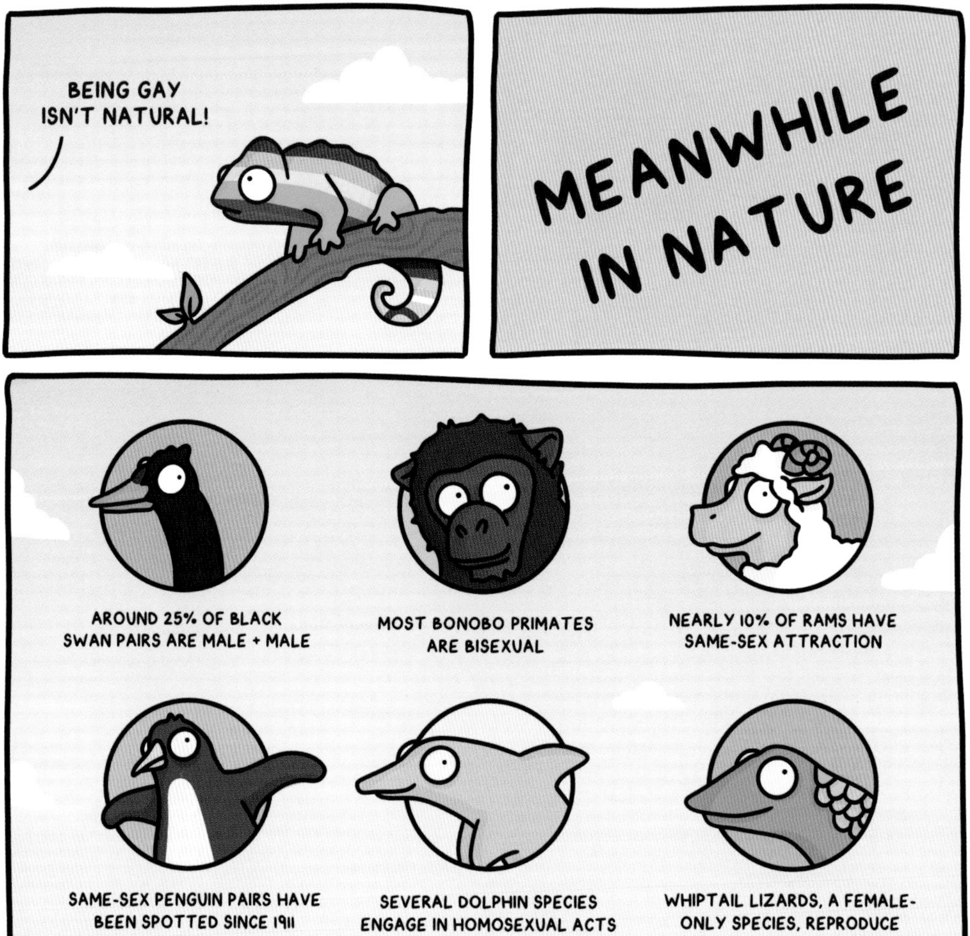
BEING GAY ISN'T NATURAL!
MEANWHILE IN NATURE
AROUND 25% OF BLACK SWAN PAIRS ARE MALE + MALE
MOST BONOBO PRIMATES ARE BISEXUAL
NEARLY 10% OF RAMS HAVE SAME-SEX ATTRACTION
SAME-SEX PENGUIN PAIRS HAVE BEEN SPOTTED SINCE 1911
SEVERAL DOLPHIN SPECIES ENGAGE IN HOMOSEXUAL ACTS
WHIPTAIL LIZARDS, A FEMALE-ONLY SPECIES, REPRODUCE

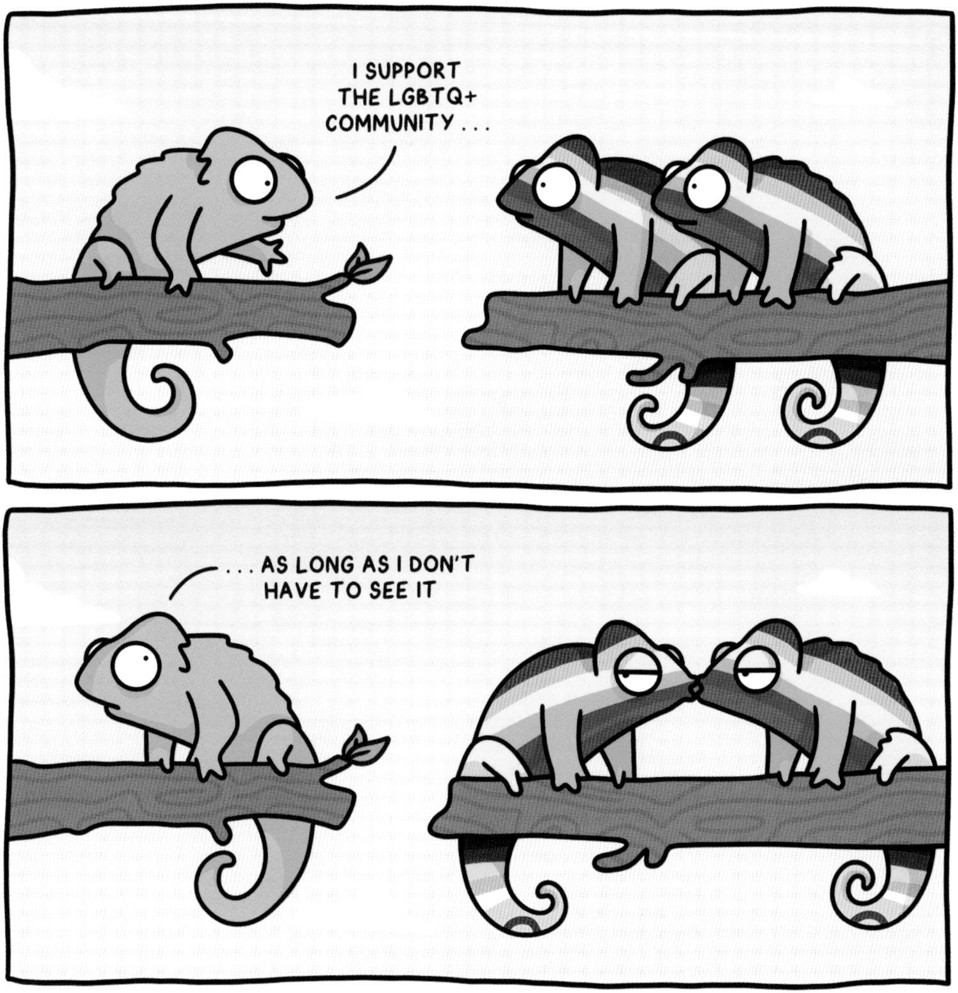
I SUPPORT THE LGBTQ+ COMMUNITY . . .
. . . AS LONG AS I DON'T HAVE TO SEE IT

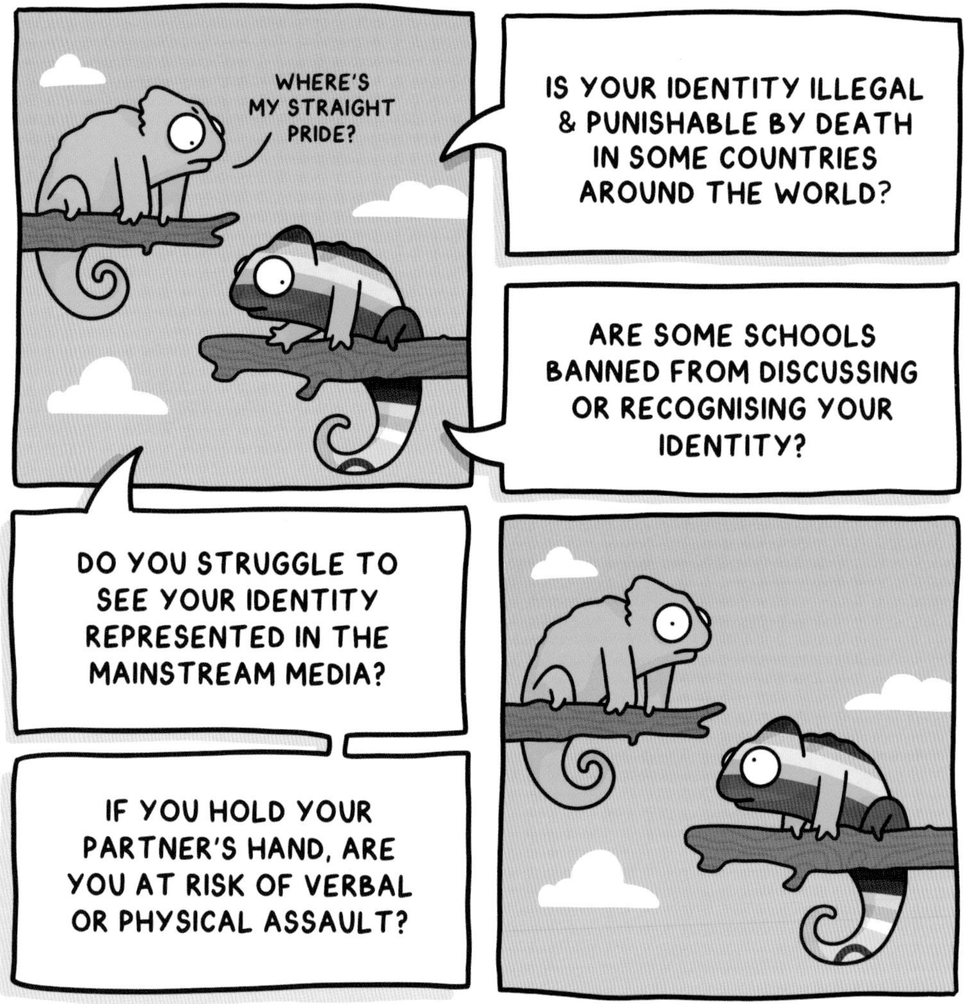
WHERE'S MY STRAIGHT PRIDE?
IS YOUR IDENTITY ILLEGAL & PUNISHABLE BY DEATH IN SOME COUNTRIES AROUND THE WORLD?
ARE SOME SCHOOLS BANNED FROM DISCUSSING OR RECOGNISING YOUR IDENTITY?
DO YOU STRUGGLE TO SEE YOUR IDENTITY REPRESENTED IN THE MAINSTREAM MEDIA?
IF YOU HOLD YOUR PARTNER'S HAND, ARE YOU AT RISK OF VERBAL OR PHYSICAL ASSAULT?

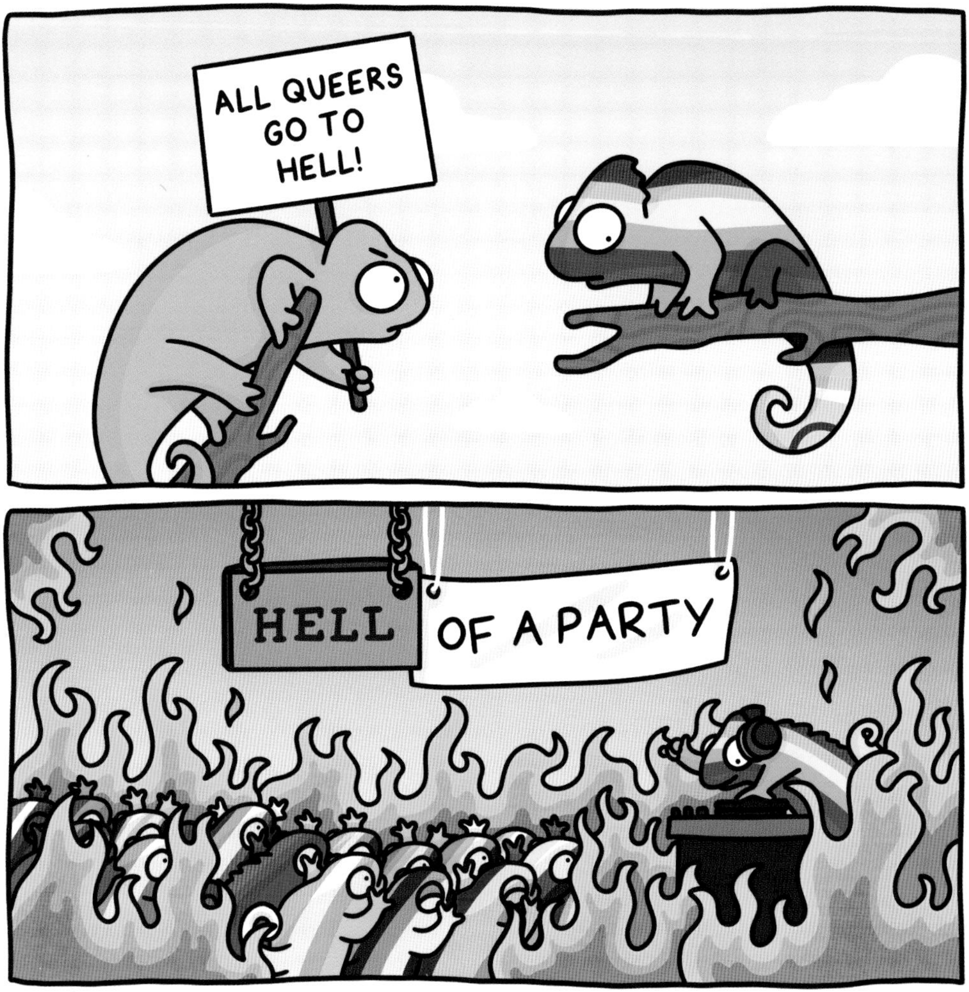
ALL QUEERS GO TO HELL!
HELL
OF A PARTY

CHAPTER 4

FUNNY...
BUT TRUE?

Warning: Some clichés may be
too close for comfort

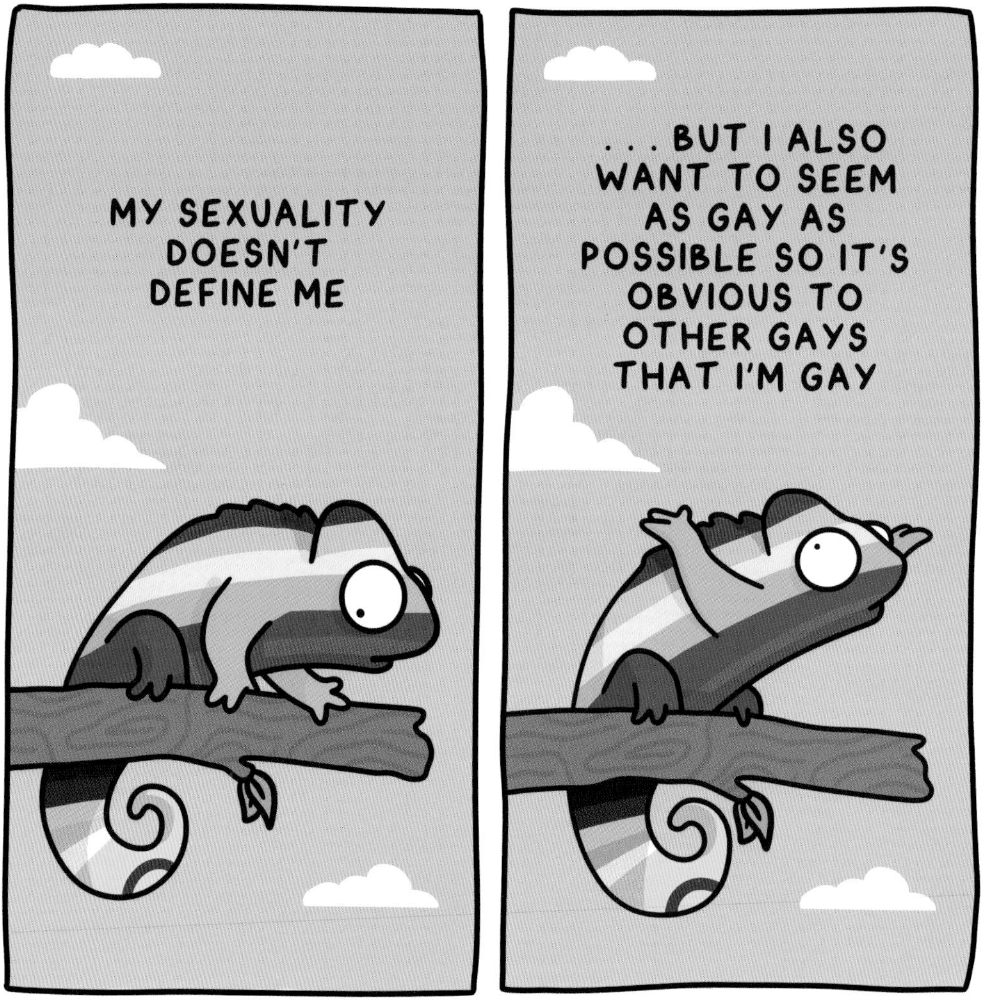
MY SEXUALITY DOESN'T DEFINE ME
. . . BUT I ALSO WANT TO SEEM AS GAY AS POSSIBLE SO IT'S OBVIOUS TO OTHER GAYS THAT I'M GAY

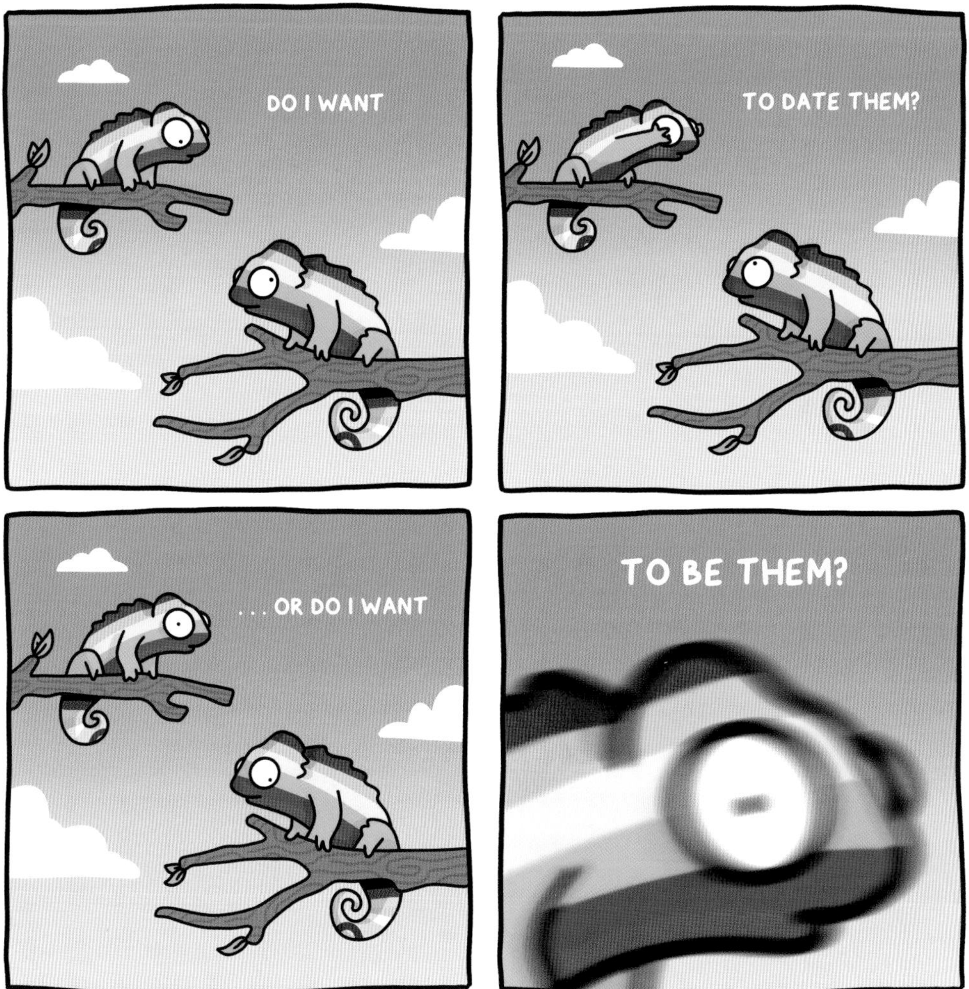
DO I WANT
TO DATE THEM?
. . . OR DO I WANT
TO BE THEM?

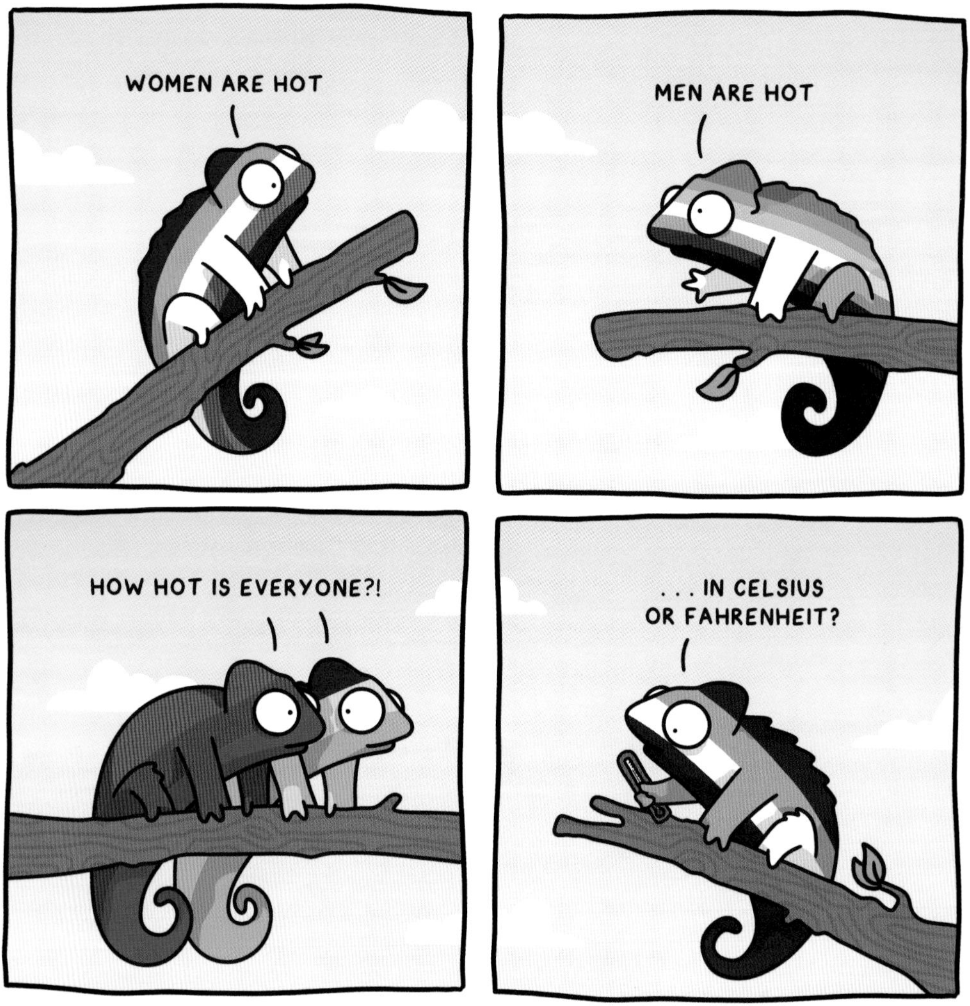
WOMEN ARE HOT
MEN ARE HOT
HOW HOT IS EVERYONE?!
. . . IN CELSIUS OR FAHRENHEIT?

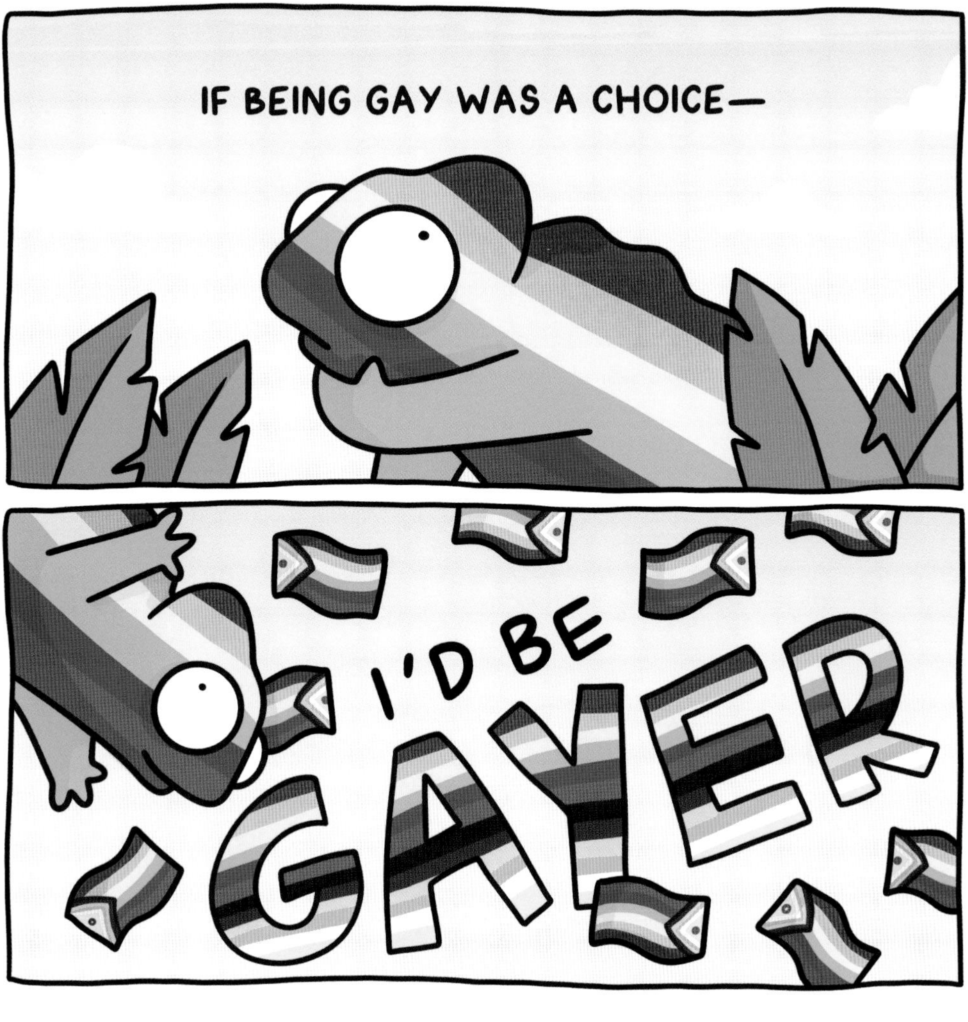
IF BEING GAY WAS A CHOICE—
I'D BE
GAYER

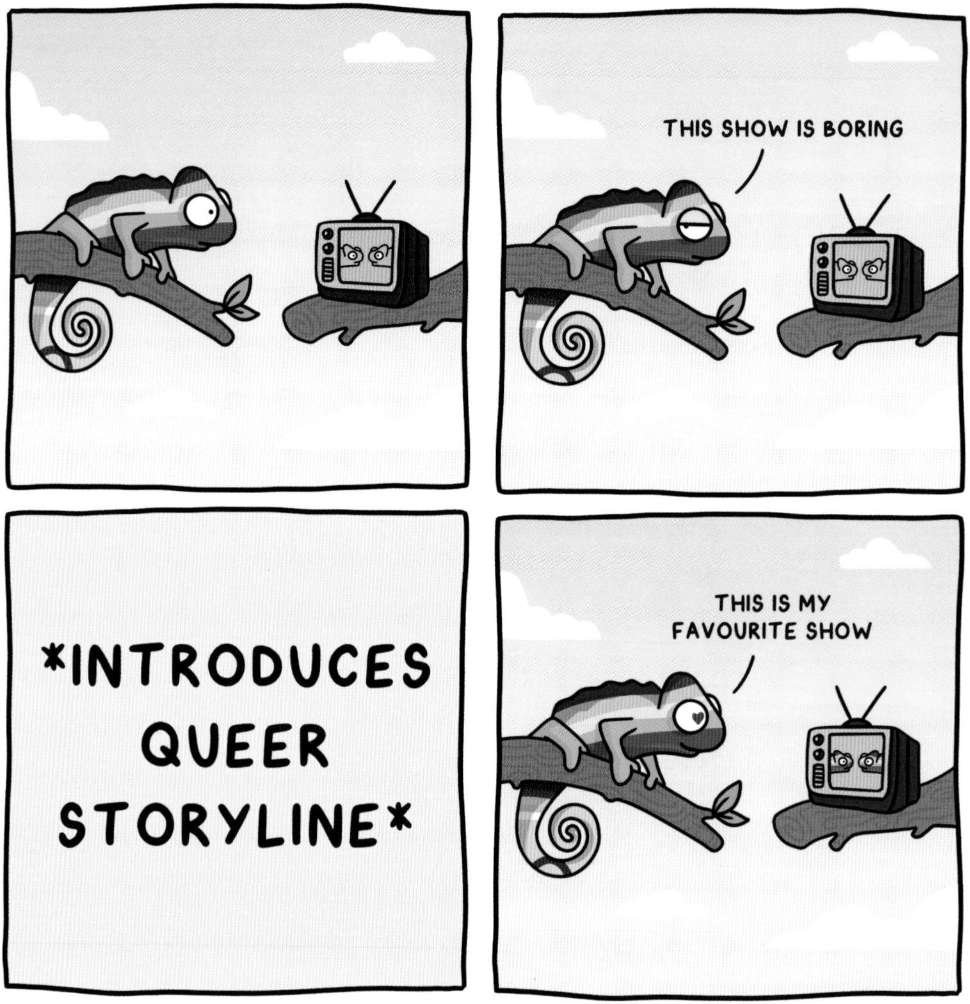
THIS SHOW IS BORING
INTRODUCES QUEER STORYLINE
THIS IS MY FAVOURITE SHOW

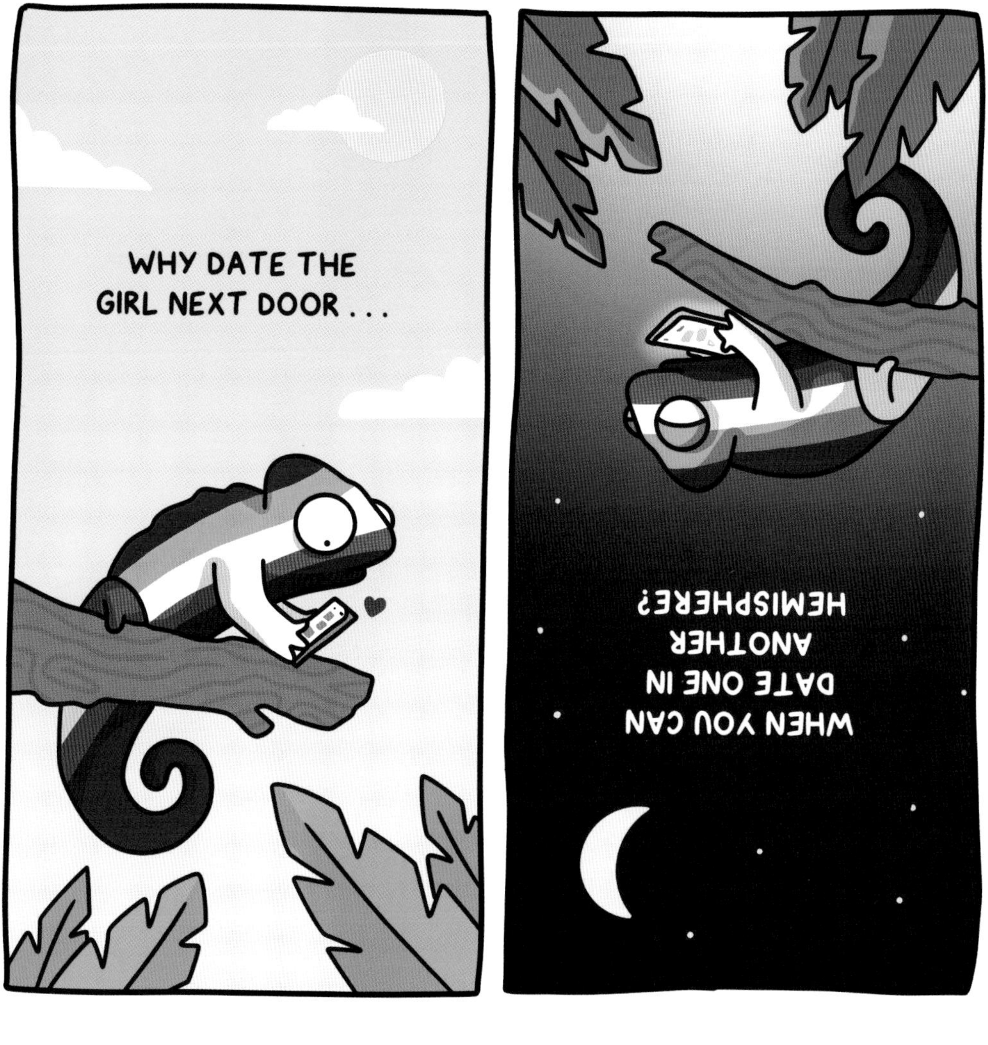
WHY DATE THE GIRL NEXT DOOR . . .
WHEN YOU CAN DATE ONE IN ANOTHER HEMISPHERE?

I'M SICK OF GAY STEREOTYPES
bzzz

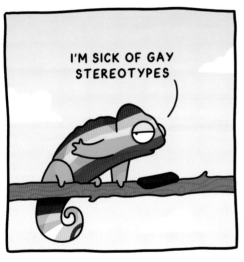

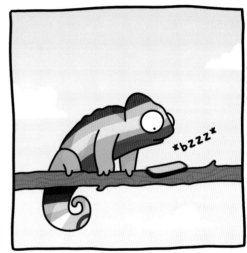

LGBTQ MEMES
@LGBTQMEMES
NO GAY HAS ALL 5:
- DRIVER'S LICENCE
- ENOUGH PLANTS
- GOOD SCHOOL MEMORIES
- HEALTHY SELF-ESTEEM
- ACCEPTING FAMILY
NO GAY HAS ALL 5:
- DRIVER'S LICENCE
- ENOUGH PLANTS
- GOOD SCHOOL MEMORIES
- HEALTHY SELF-ESTEEM
- ACCEPTING FAMILY
. . . LOL IT ME

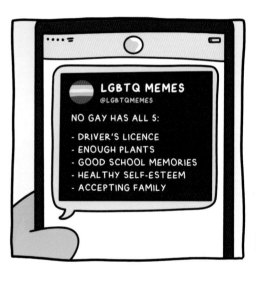

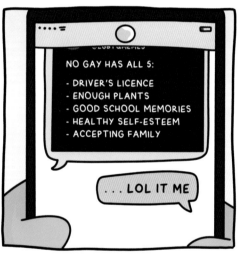

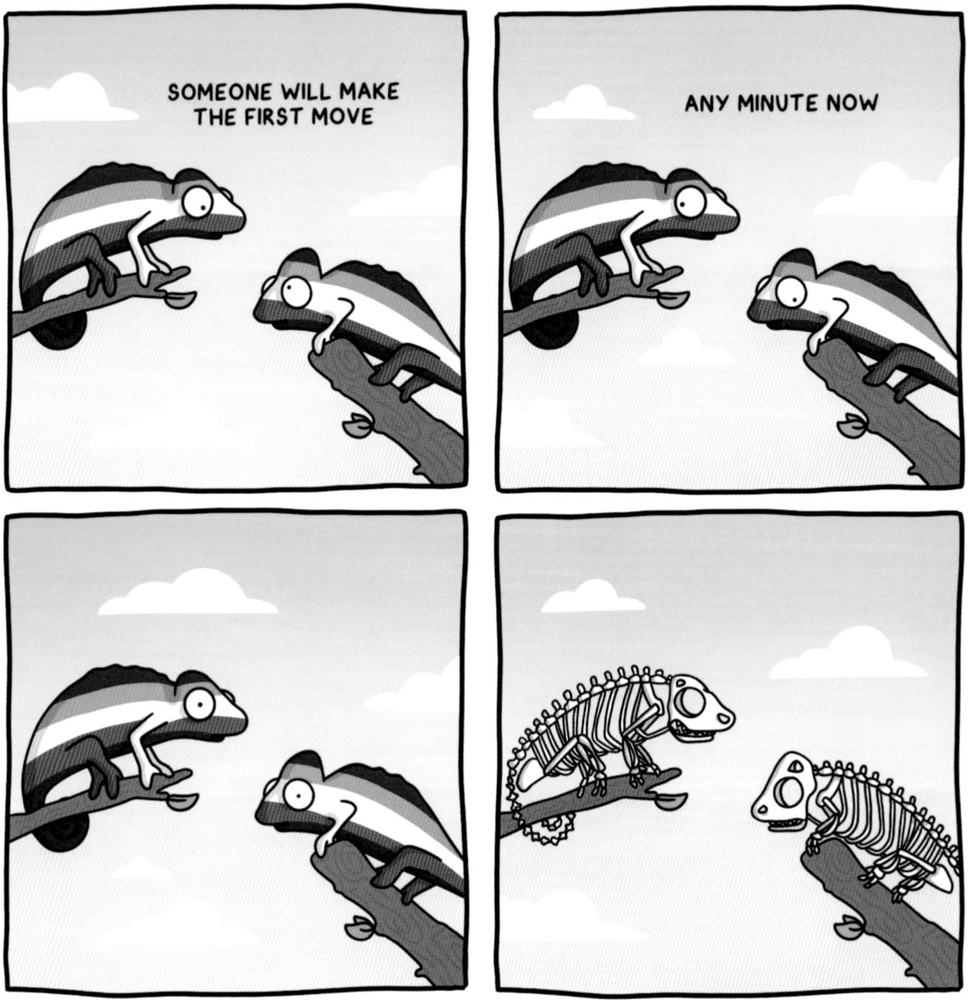
SOMEONE WILL MAKE THE FIRST MOVE
ANY MINUTE NOW

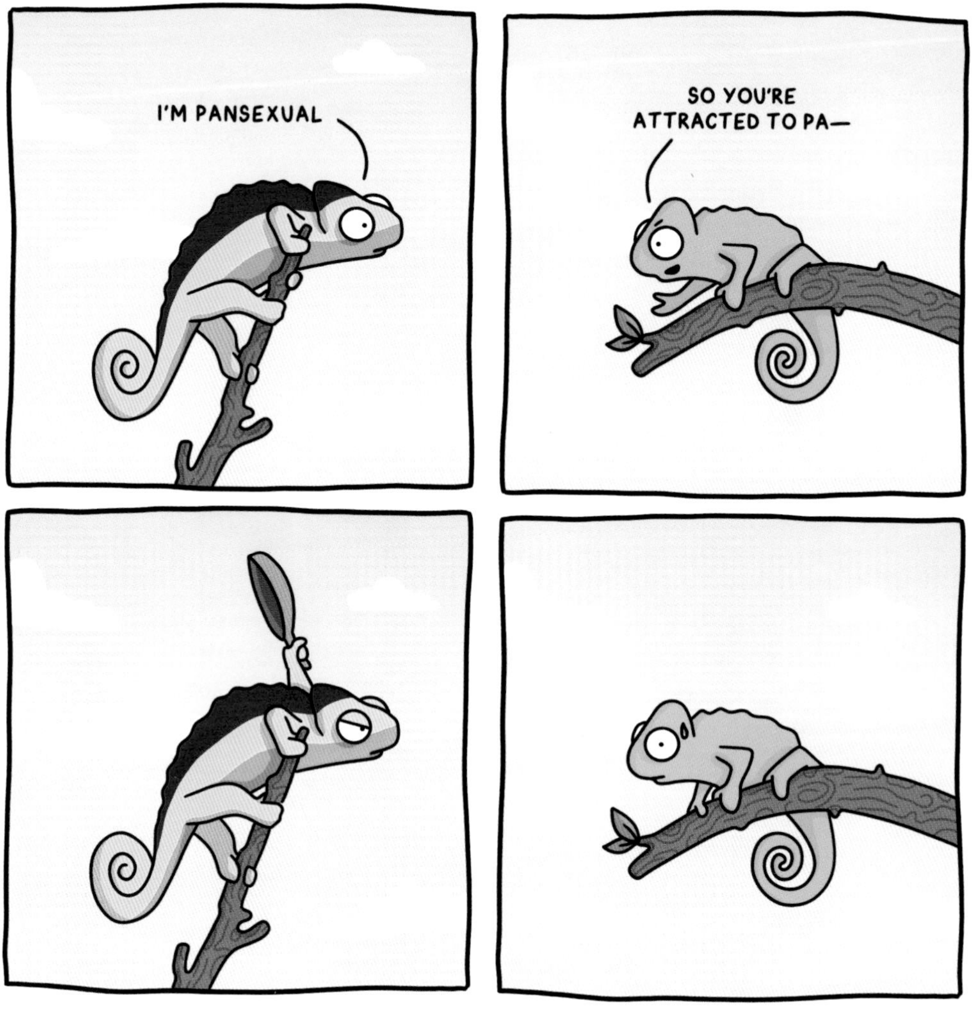
I'M PANSEXUAL
SO YOU'RE ATTRACTED TO PA—

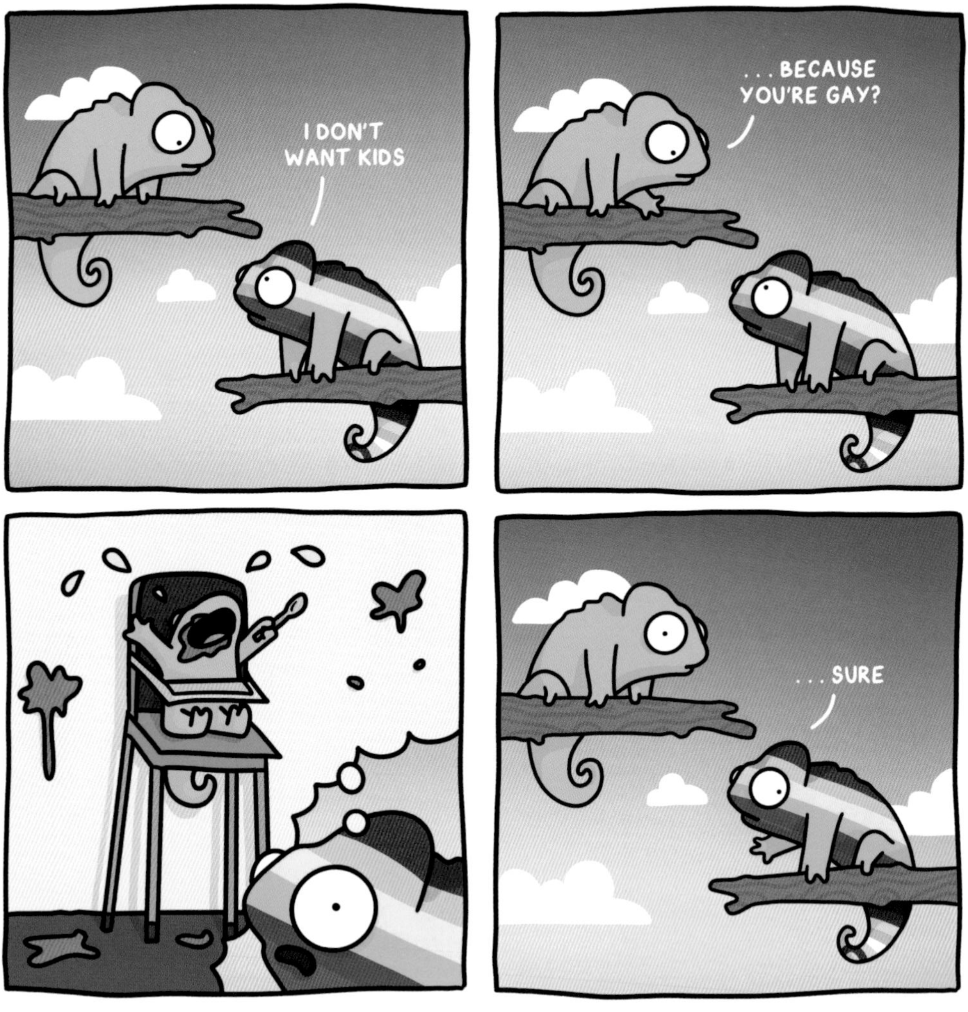
I DON'T WANT KIDS
. . . BECAUSE YOU'RE GAY?
. . . SURE

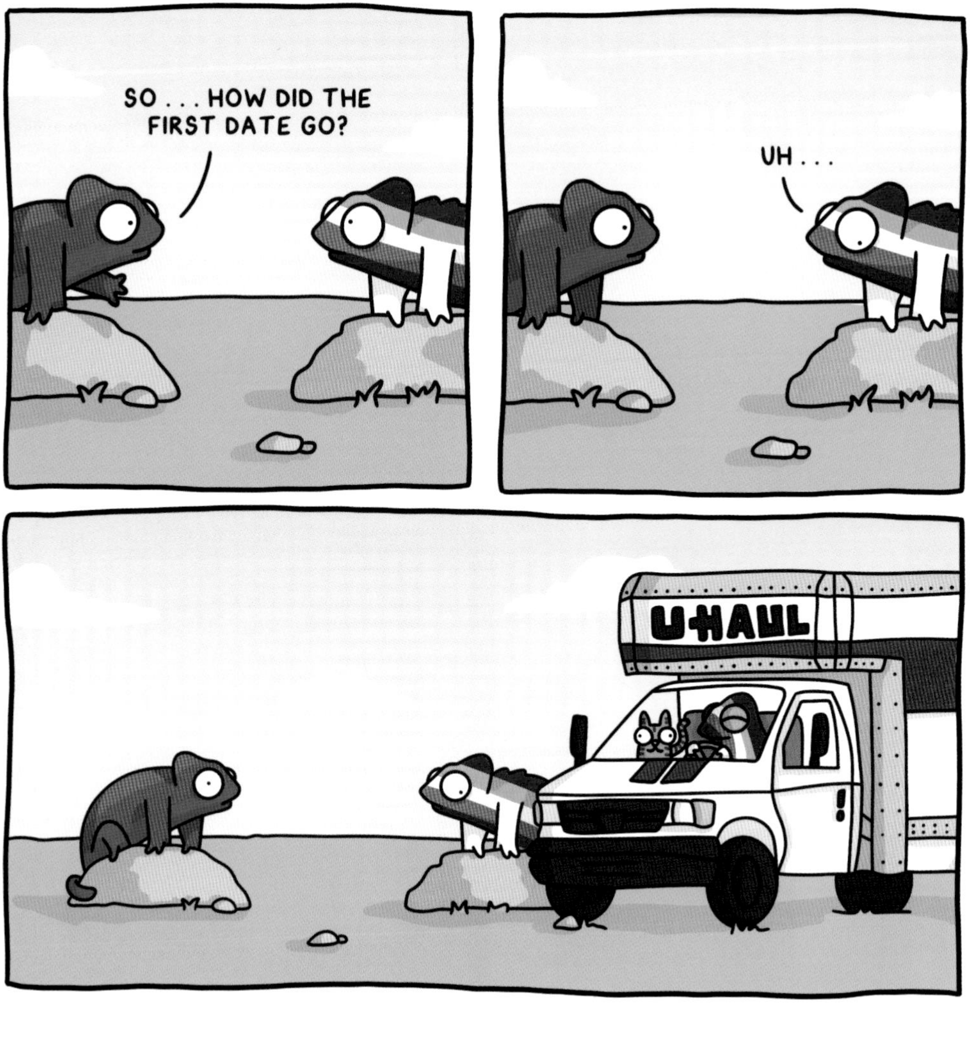
SO . . . HOW DID THE FIRST DATE GO?
UH . . .
U-HAUL

HI
IS SHE FLIRTING WITH ME?!
WHAT IF SHE'S JUST FRIENDLY?

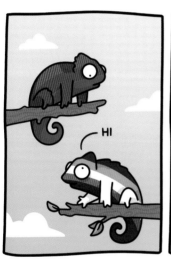

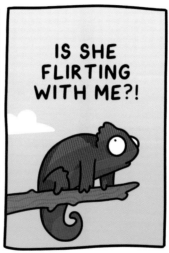

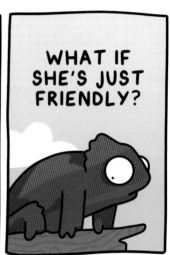

HOW DO I LET HER KNOW I'M BISEXUAL?
. . . . I WONDER WHAT HER STAR SIGN IS
OH NO

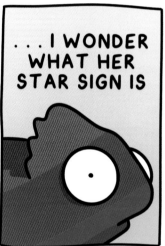

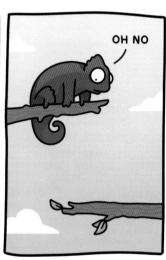

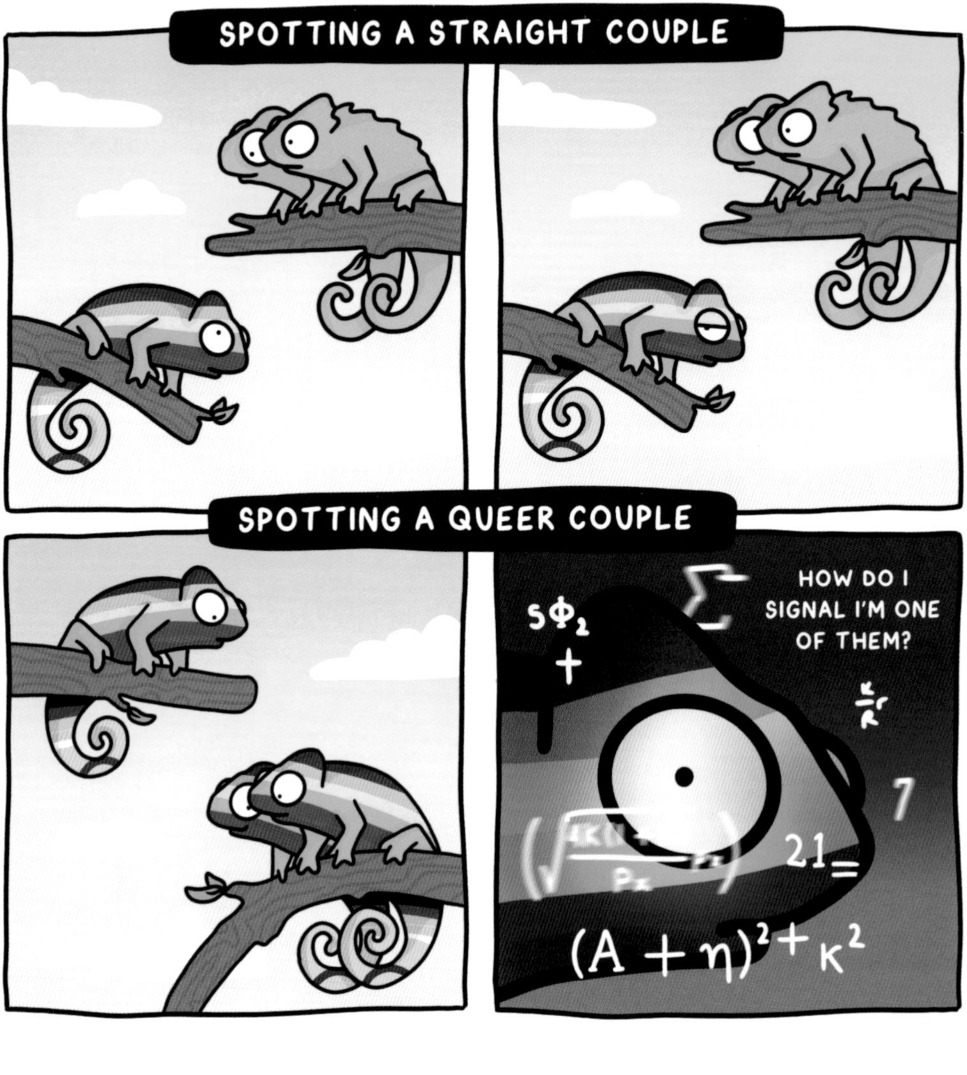
SPOTTING A STRAIGHT COUPLE
SPOTTING A QUEER COUPLE
HOW DO I SIGNAL I'M ONE OF THEM?
$5\Phi_2$
$(A+\eta)^2+\kappa^2$

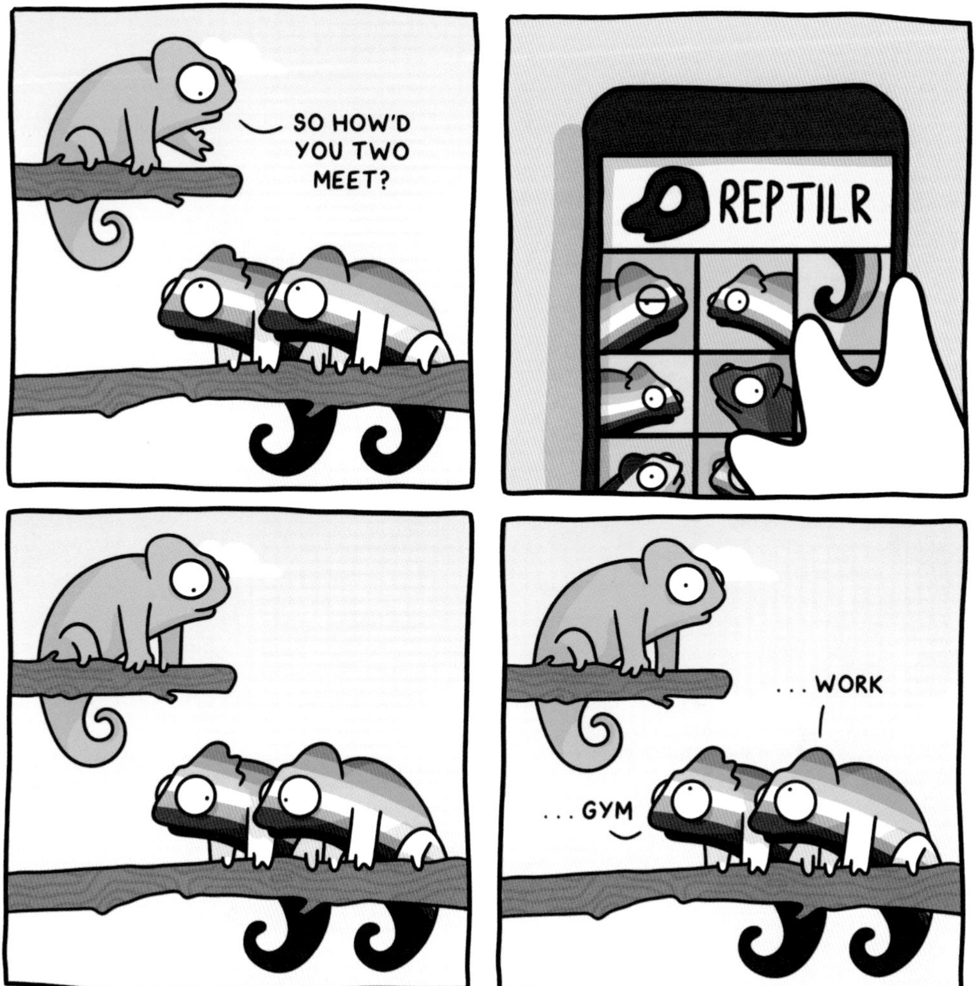
SO HOW'D YOU TWO MEET?
REPTILR
. . . GYM
. . . WORK

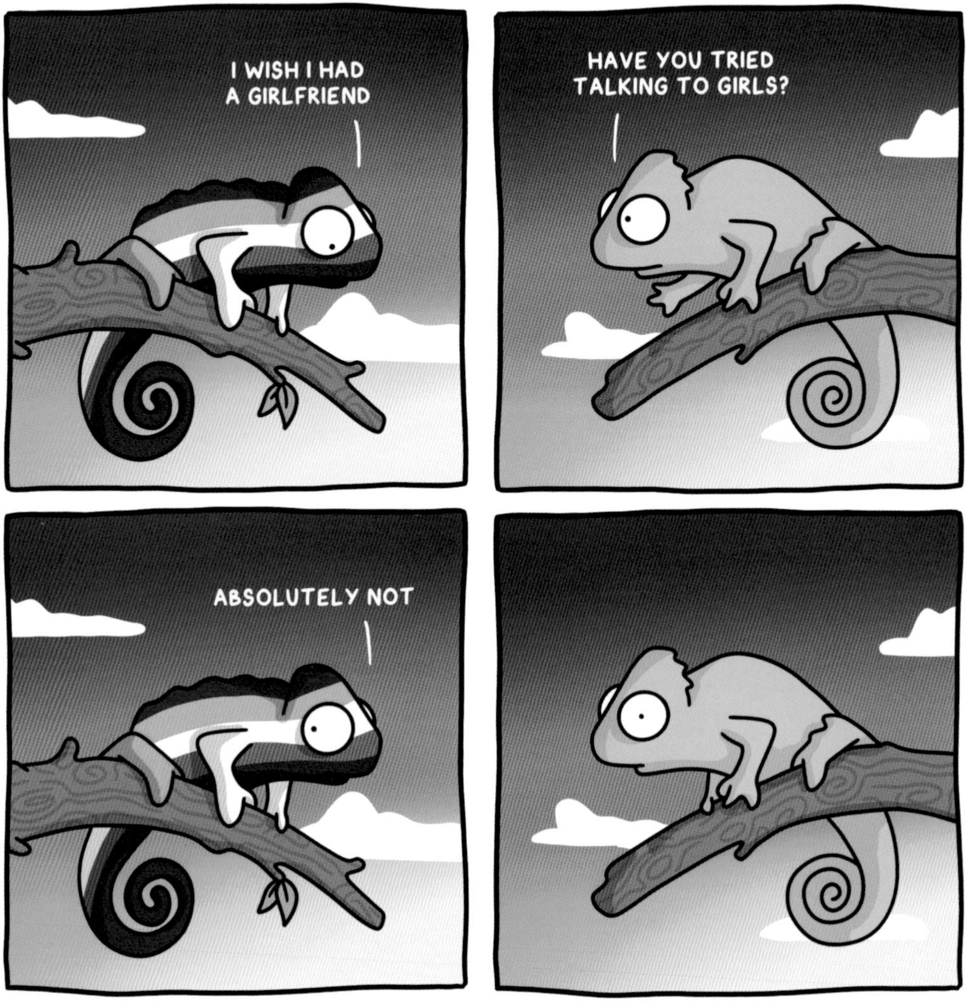
I WISH I HAD A GIRLFRIEND
HAVE YOU TRIED TALKING TO GIRLS?
ABSOLUTELY NOT

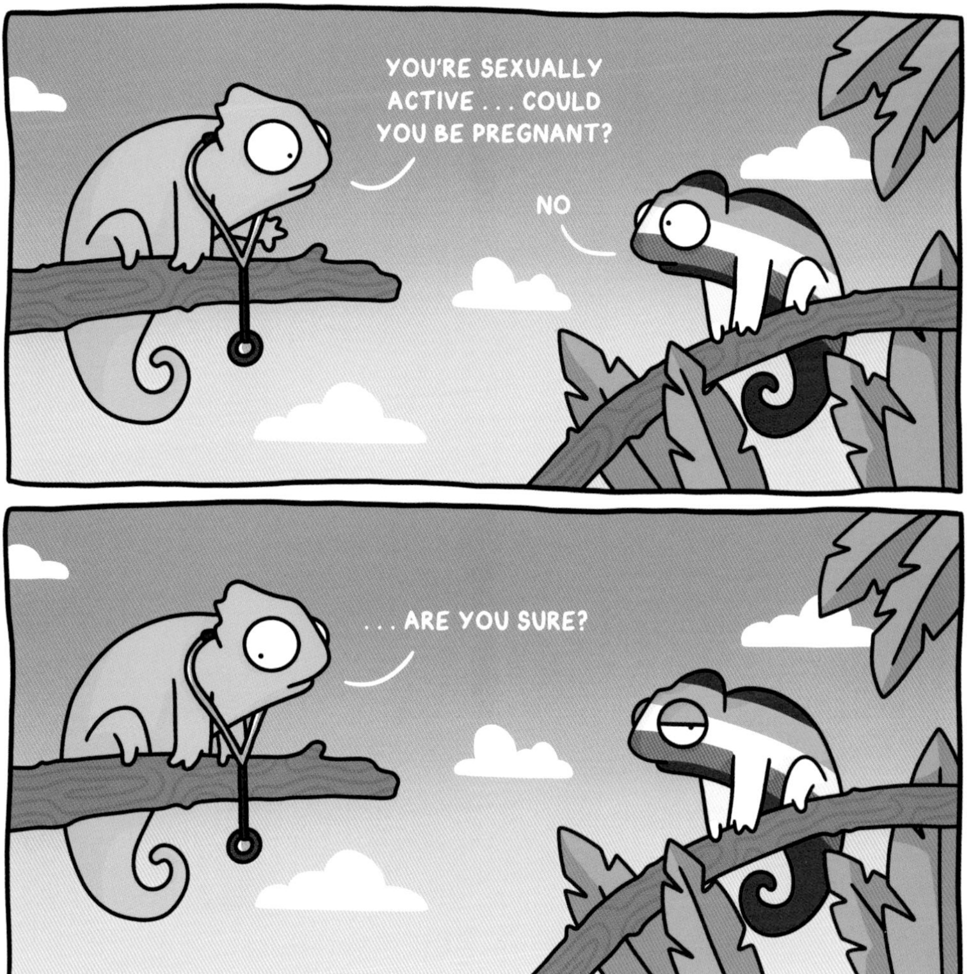
YOU'RE SEXUALLY ACTIVE . . . COULD YOU BE PREGNANT?
NO
. . . ARE YOU SURE?

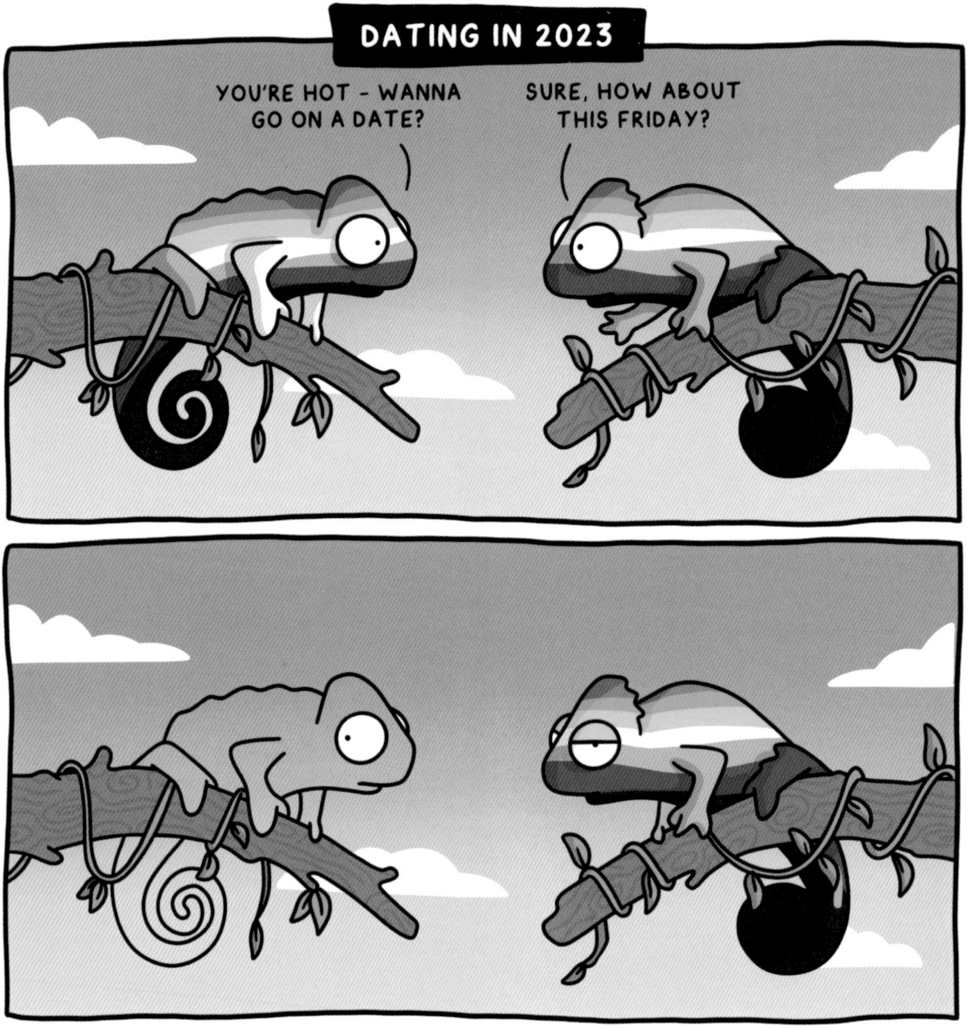
DATING IN 2023
YOU'RE HOT - WANNA GO ON A DATE?
SURE, HOW ABOUT THIS FRIDAY?

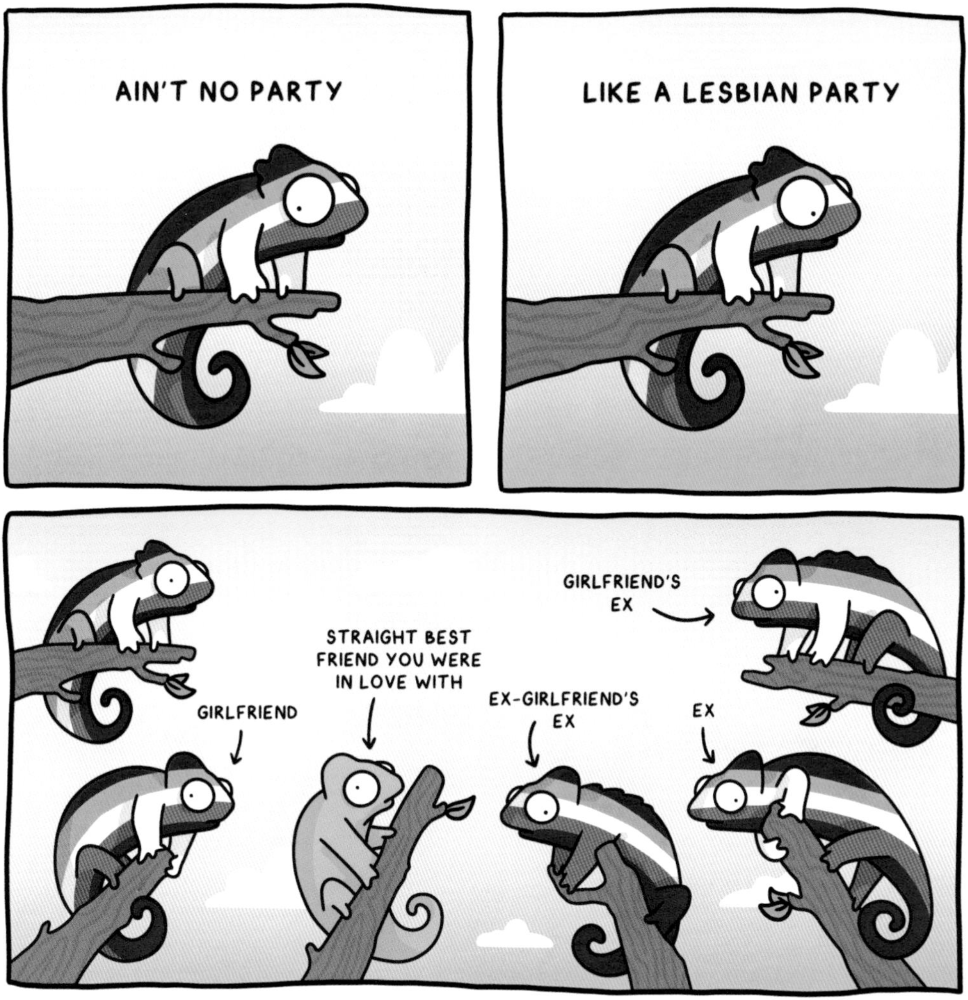
AIN'T NO PARTY
LIKE A LESBIAN PARTY
GIRLFRIEND
STRAIGHT BEST FRIEND YOU WERE IN LOVE WITH
EX-GIRLFRIEND'S EX
GIRLFRIEND'S EX
EX

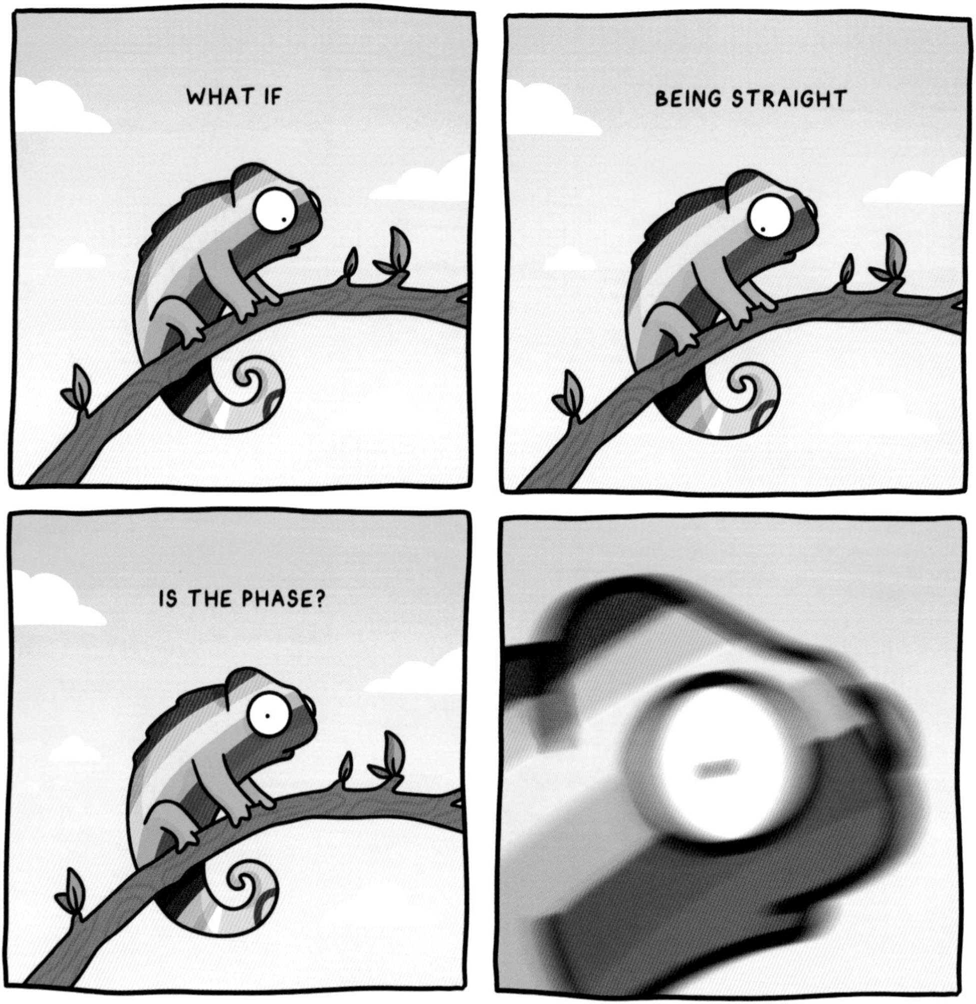
WHAT IF
BEING STRAIGHT
IS THE PHASE?

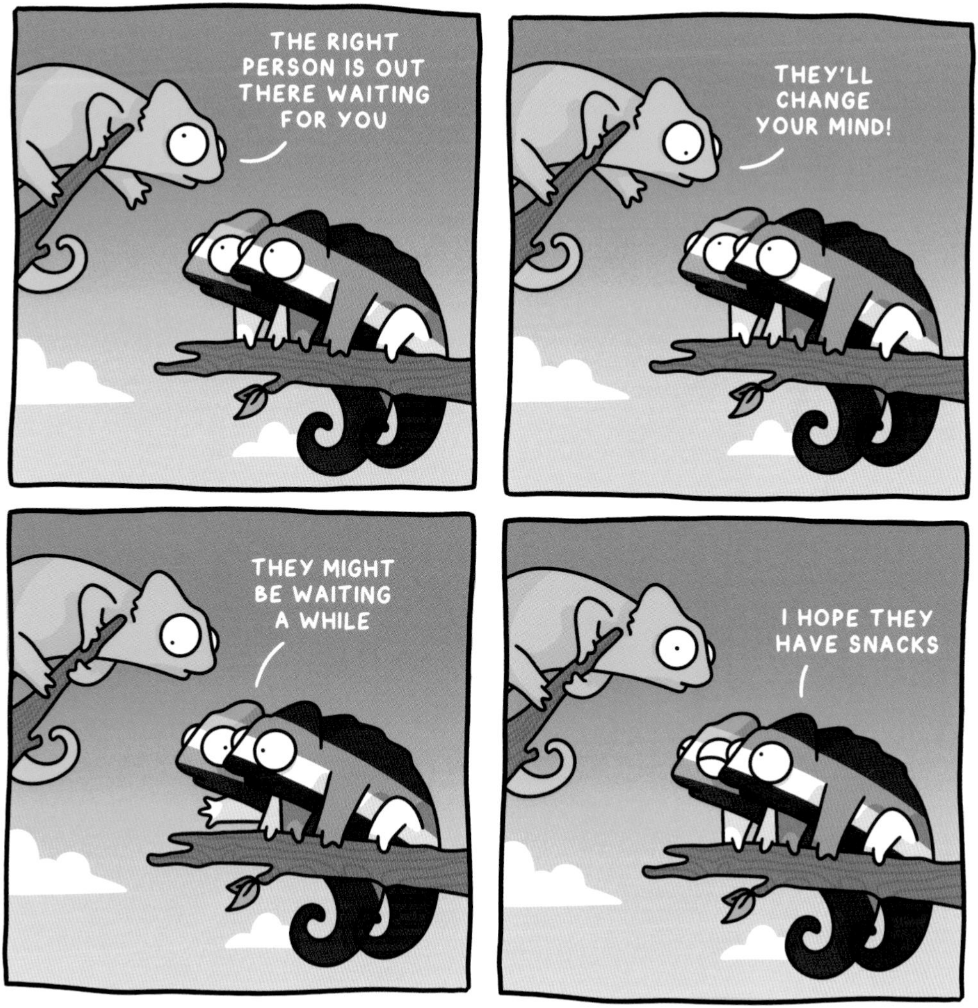
THE RIGHT PERSON IS OUT THERE WAITING FOR YOU
THEY'LL CHANGE YOUR MIND!
THEY MIGHT BE WAITING A WHILE
I HOPE THEY HAVE SNACKS

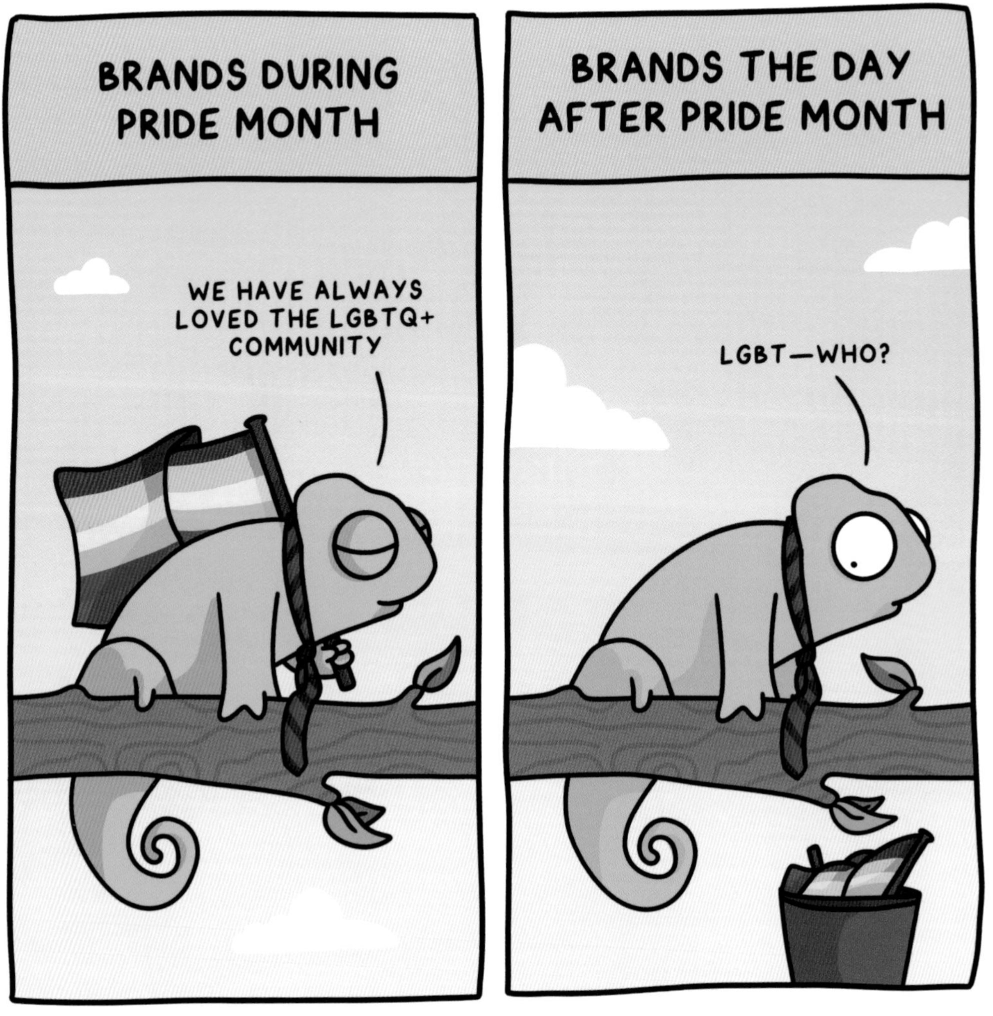
BRANDS DURING PRIDE MONTH
WE HAVE ALWAYS LOVED THE LGBTQ+ COMMUNITY
BRANDS THE DAY AFTER PRIDE MONTH
LGBT—WHO?

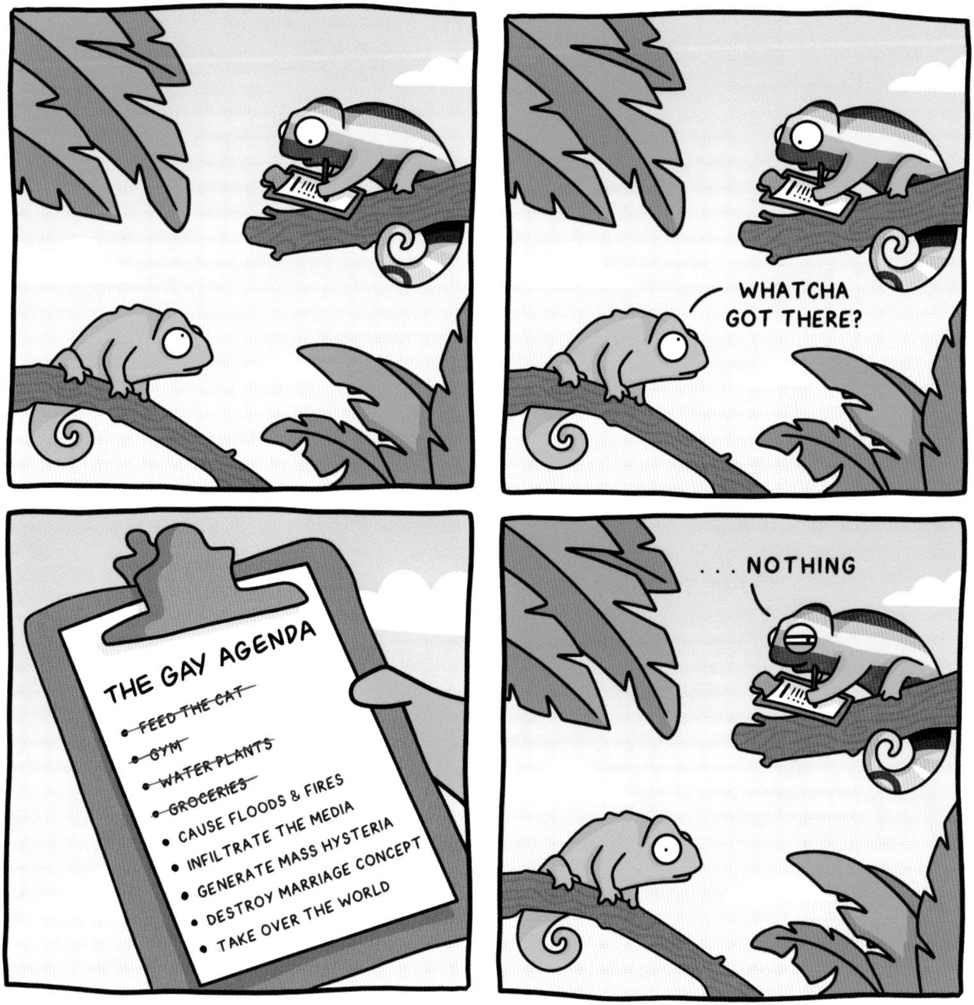
WHATCHA GOT THERE?
THE GAY AGENDA
FEED THE CAT
GYM
WATER PLANTS
GROCERIES
CAUSE FLOODS & FIRES
INFILTRATE THE MEDIA
GENERATE MASS HYSTERIA
DESTROY MARRIAGE CONCEPT
TAKE OVER THE WORLD
. . . NOTHING

CHAPTER 5

BEYOND THE BINARY

Celebrating the beautiful gender spectrum.
Who needs boxes anyway?

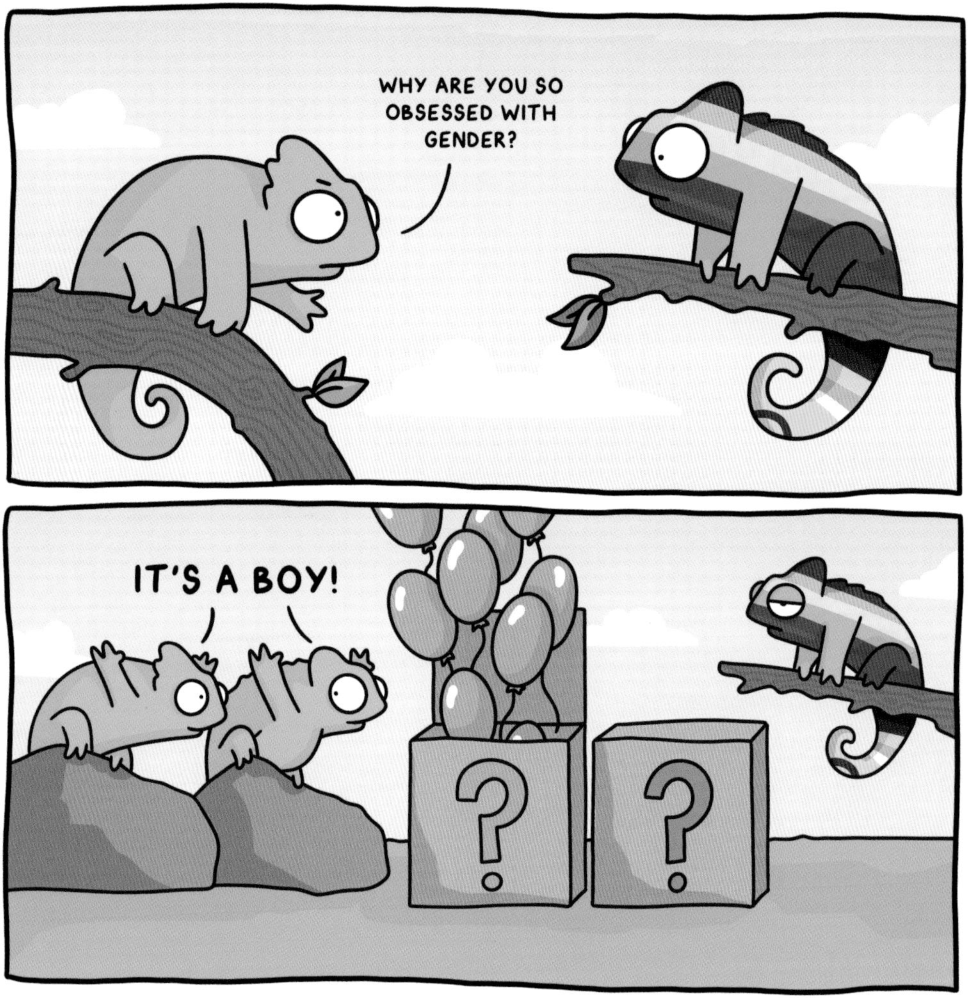
WHY ARE YOU SO OBSESSED WITH GENDER?
IT'S A BOY!

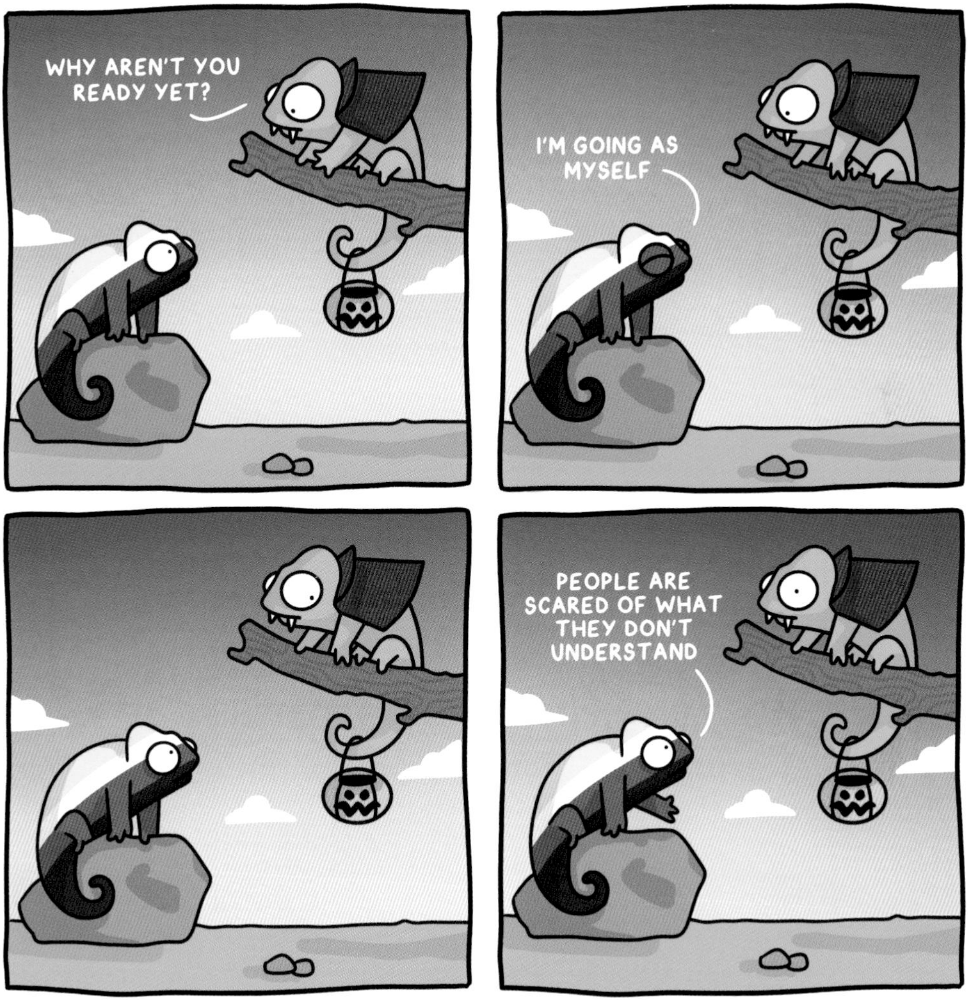
WHY AREN'T YOU READY YET?
I'M GOING AS MYSELF
PEOPLE ARE SCARED OF WHAT THEY DON'T UNDERSTAND

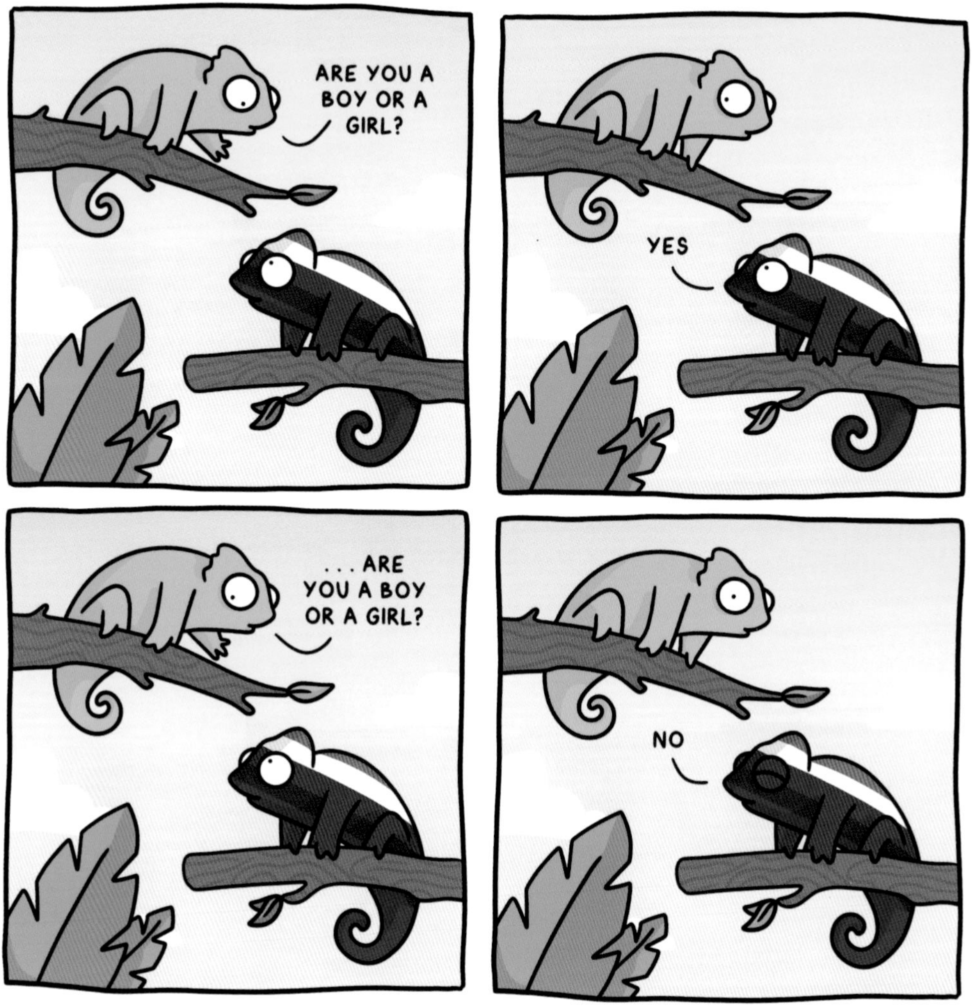
ARE YOU A BOY OR A GIRL?
YES
. . . ARE YOU A BOY OR A GIRL?
NO

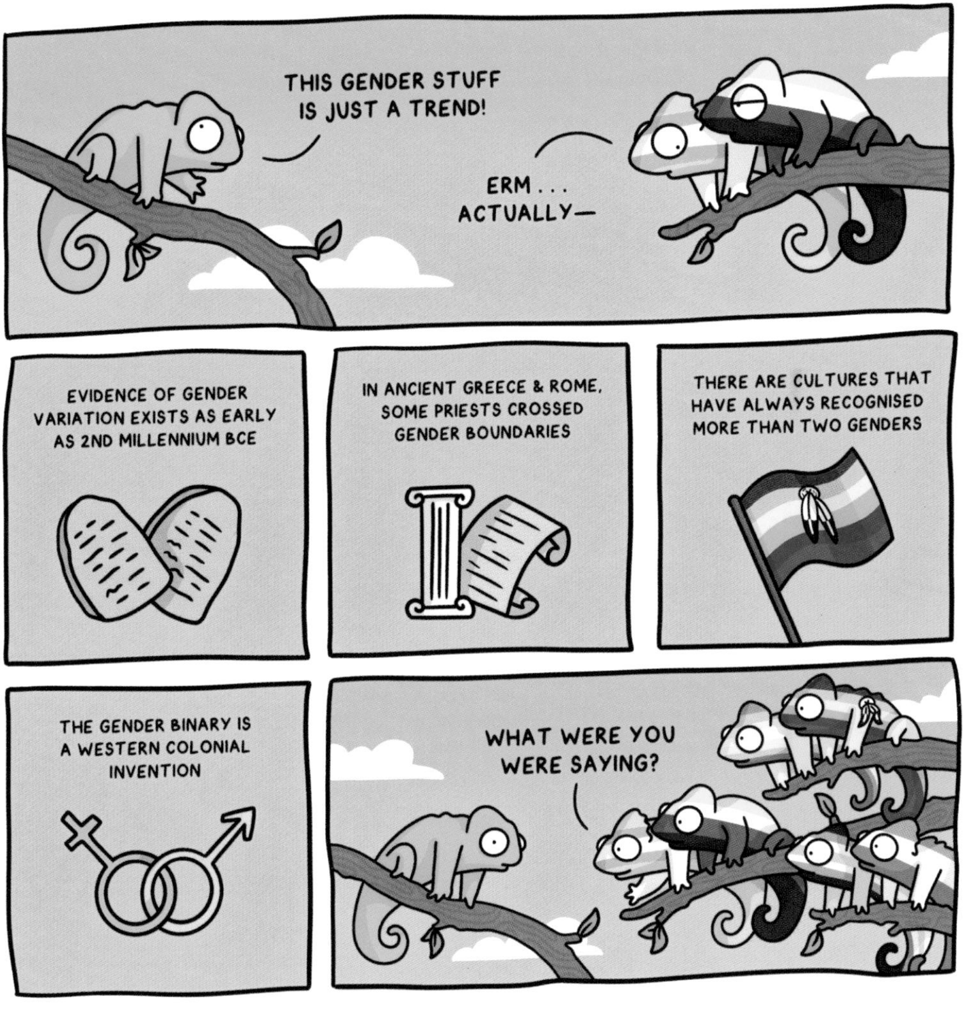

THIS GENDER STUFF IS JUST A TREND!
ERM . . . ACTUALLY—
EVIDENCE OF GENDER VARIATION EXISTS AS EARLY AS 2ND MILLENNIUM BCE
IN ANCIENT GREECE & ROME, SOME PRIESTS CROSSED GENDER BOUNDARIES
THERE ARE CULTURES THAT HAVE ALWAYS RECOGNISED MORE THAN TWO GENDERS
THE GENDER BINARY IS A WESTERN COLONIAL INVENTION
WHAT WERE YOU WERE SAYING?

TRANS KIDS
DESERVE

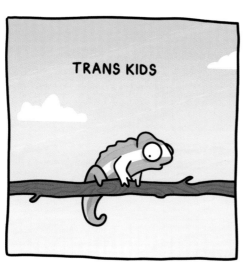

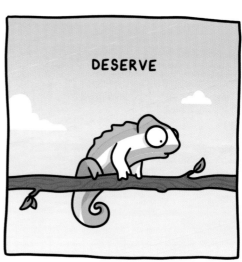

TO BECOME

HAPPY ADULTS

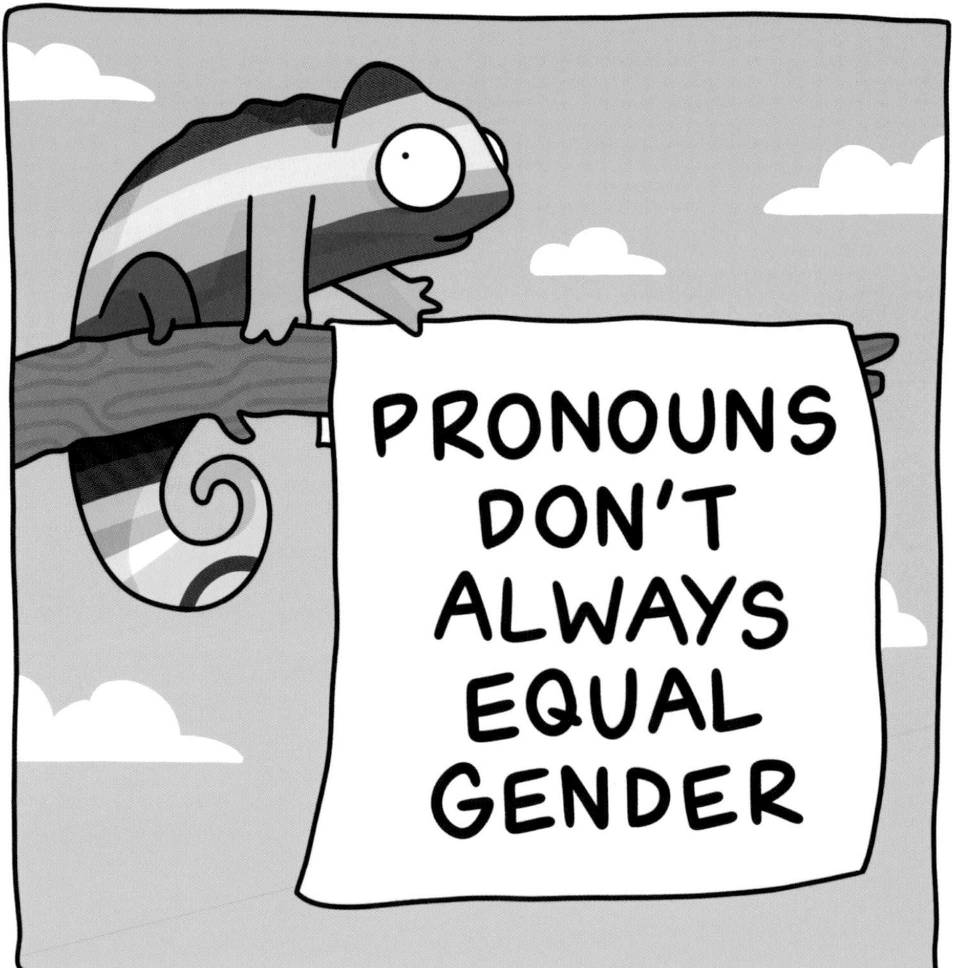
PRONOUNS DON'T ALWAYS EQUAL GENDER

PRONOUNS #101

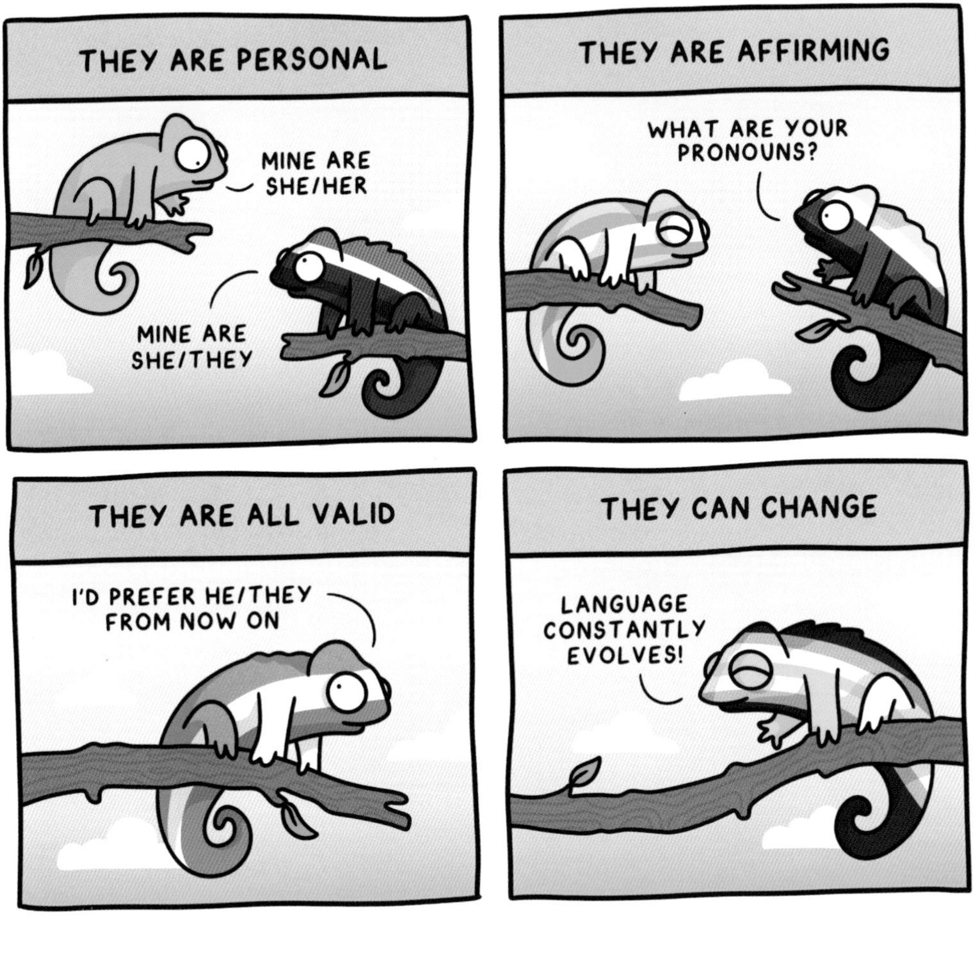
THEY ARE PERSONAL
MINE ARE SHE/HER
MINE ARE SHE/THEY
THEY ARE AFFIRMING
WHAT ARE YOUR PRONOUNS?
THEY ARE ALL VALID
I'D PREFER HE/THEY FROM NOW ON
THEY CAN CHANGE
LANGUAGE CONSTANTLY EVOLVES!

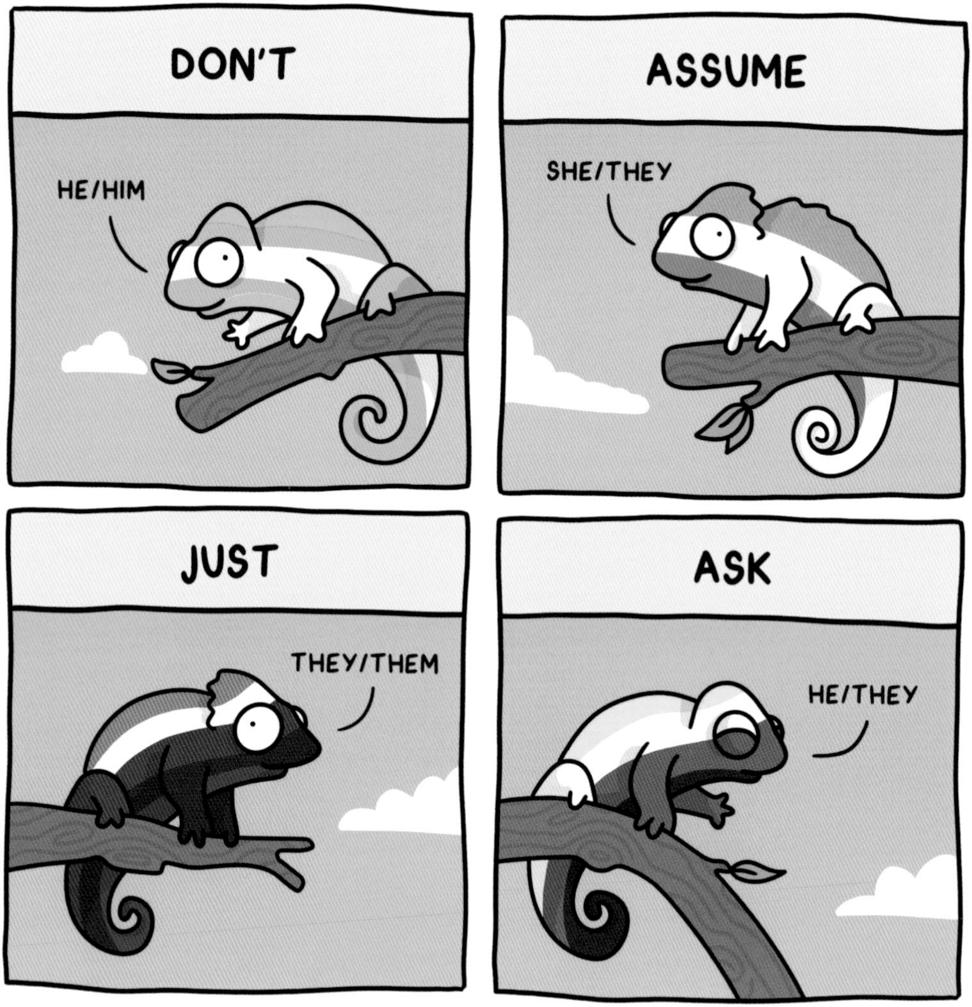
DON'T
HE/HIM
ASSUME
SHE/THEY
JUST
THEY/THEM
ASK
HE/THEY

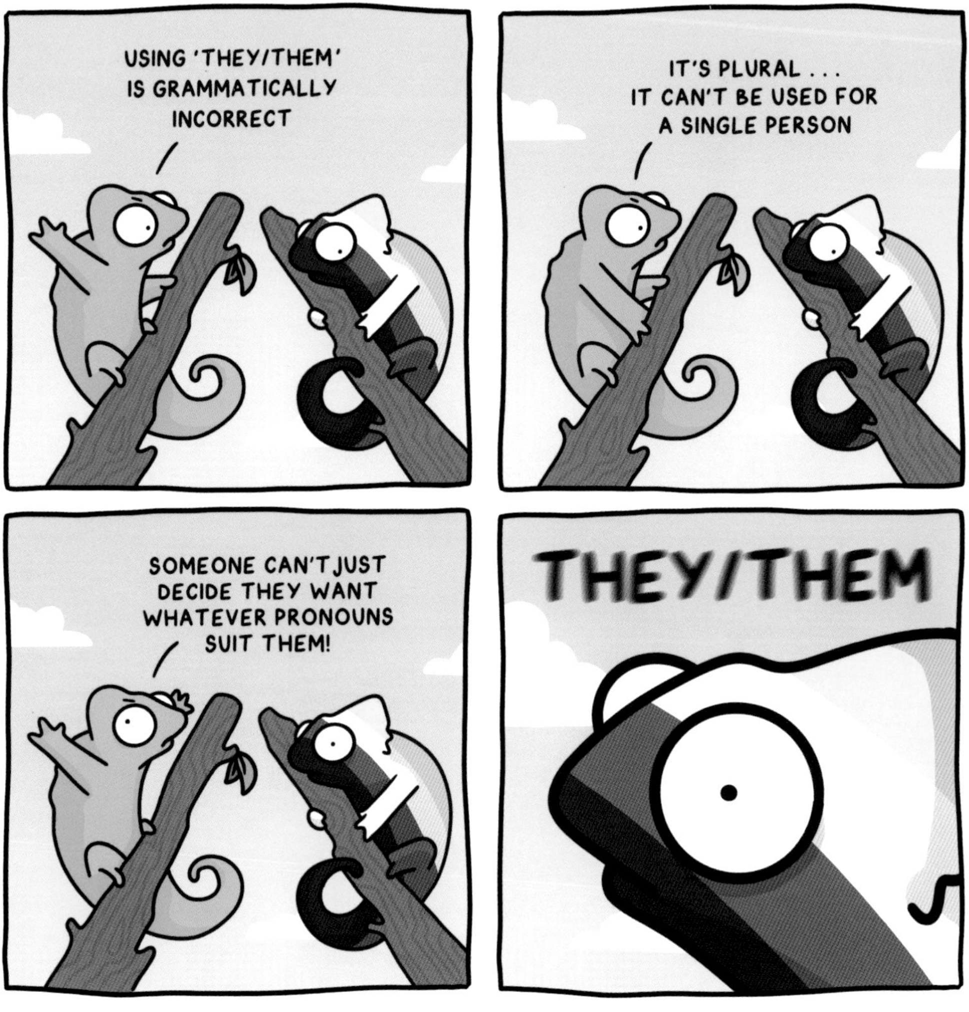
USING 'THEY/THEM' IS GRAMMATICALLY INCORRECT
IT'S PLURAL . . . IT CAN'T BE USED FOR A SINGLE PERSON
SOMEONE CAN'T JUST DECIDE THEY WANT WHATEVER PRONOUNS SUIT THEM!
THEY/THEM

THINGS THAT HAVE NO GENDER

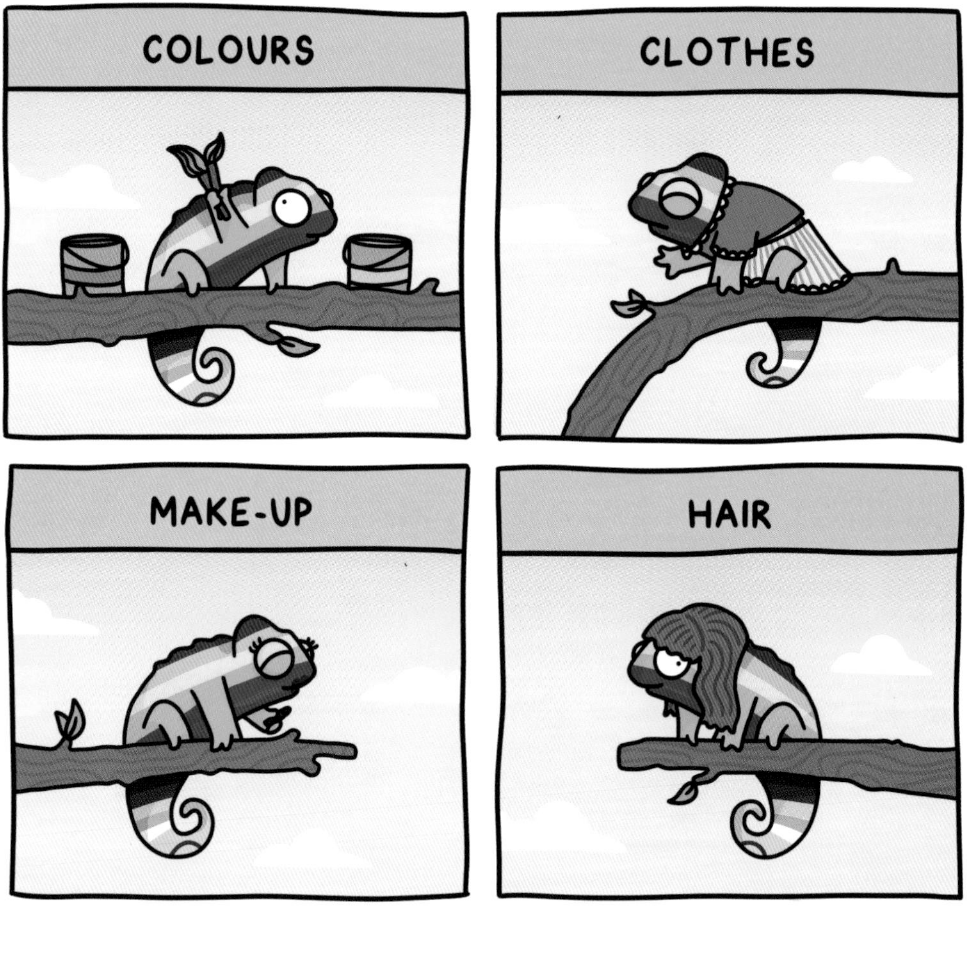
COLOURS
CLOTHES
MAKE-UP
HAIR

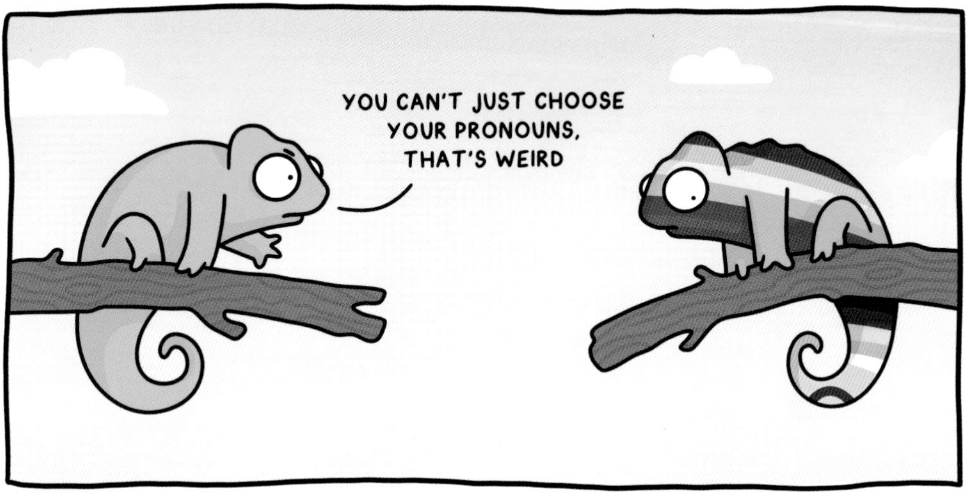
YOU CAN'T JUST CHOOSE YOUR PRONOUNS, THAT'S WEIRD

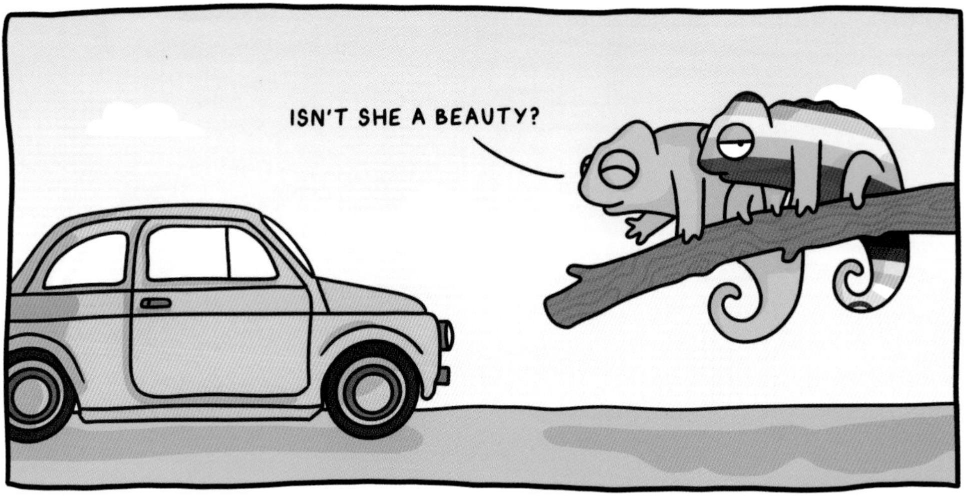
ISN'T SHE A BEAUTY?

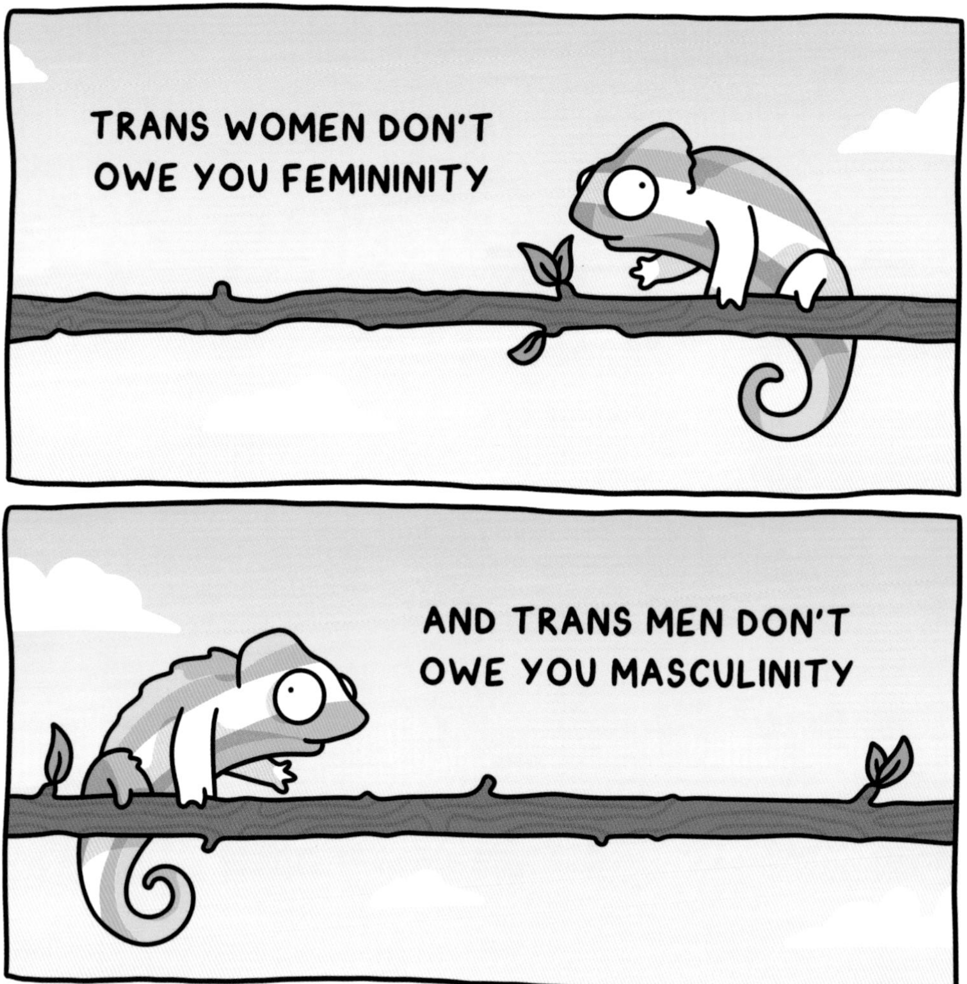
TRANS WOMEN DON'T OWE YOU FEMININITY
AND TRANS MEN DON'T OWE YOU MASCULINITY

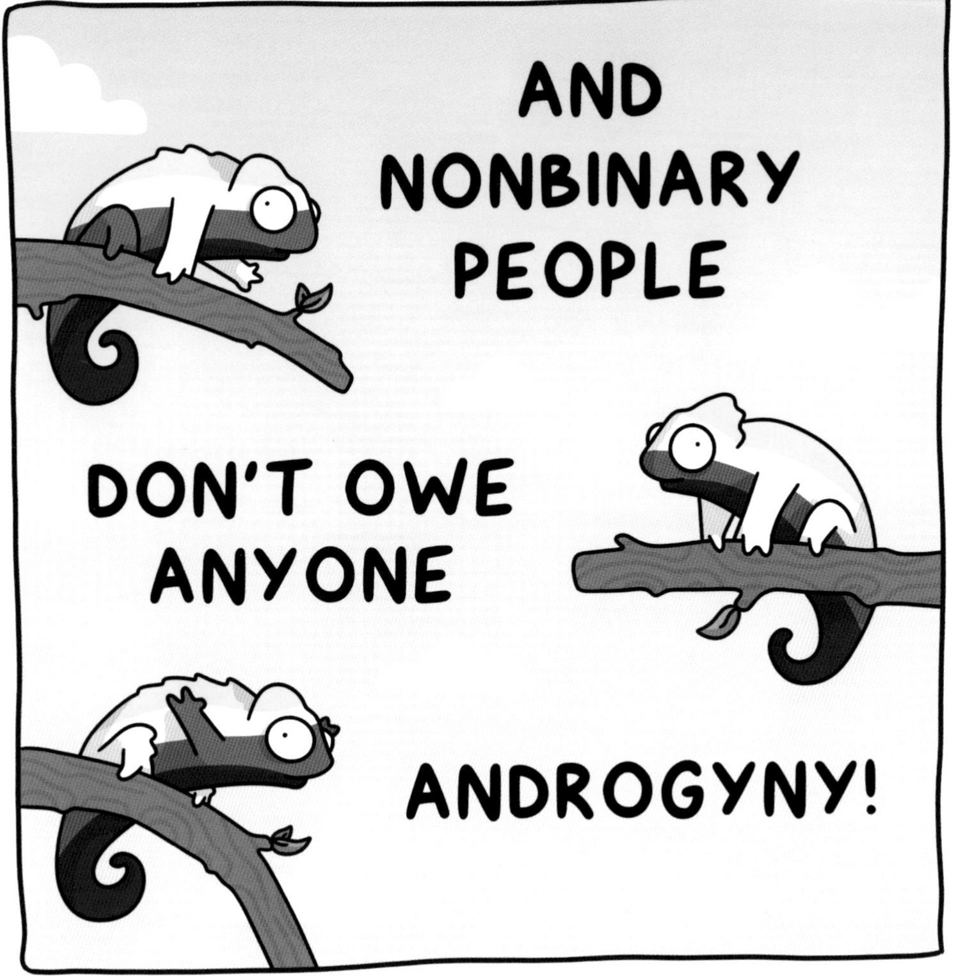
AND
NONBINARY
PEOPLE
DON'T OWE
ANYONE
ANDROGYNY!

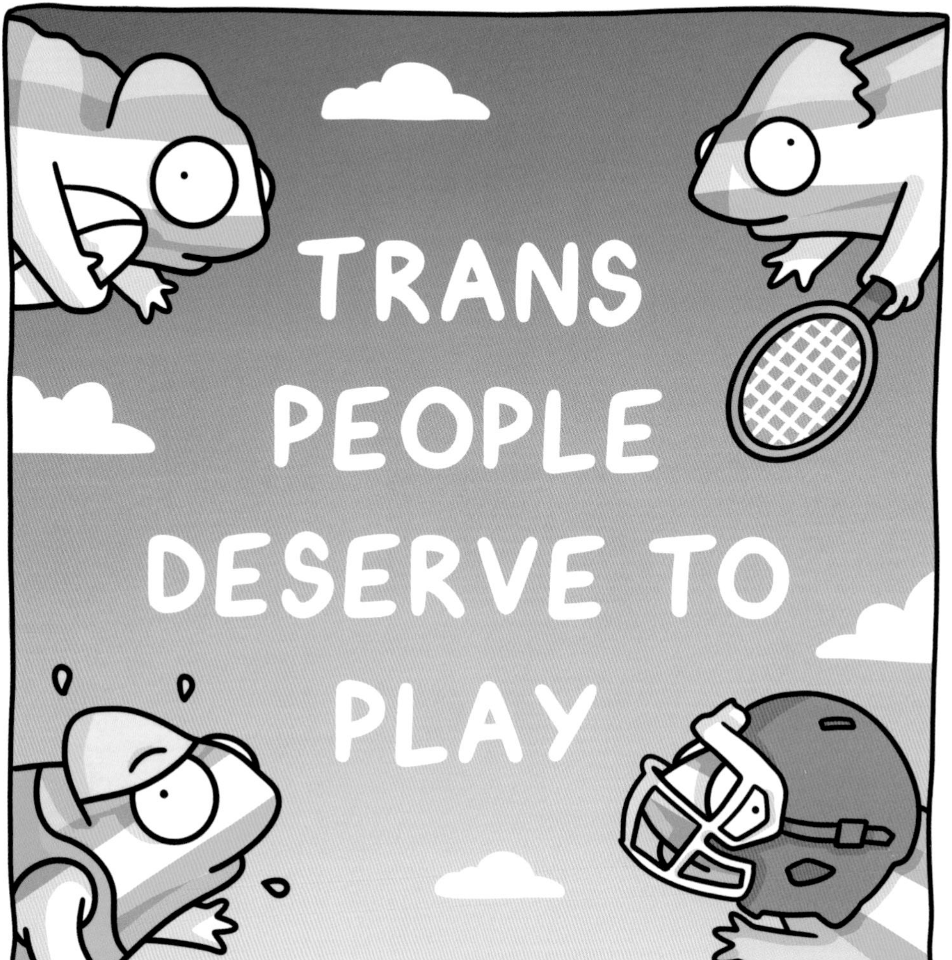
TRANS
PEOPLE
DESERVE TO
PLAY

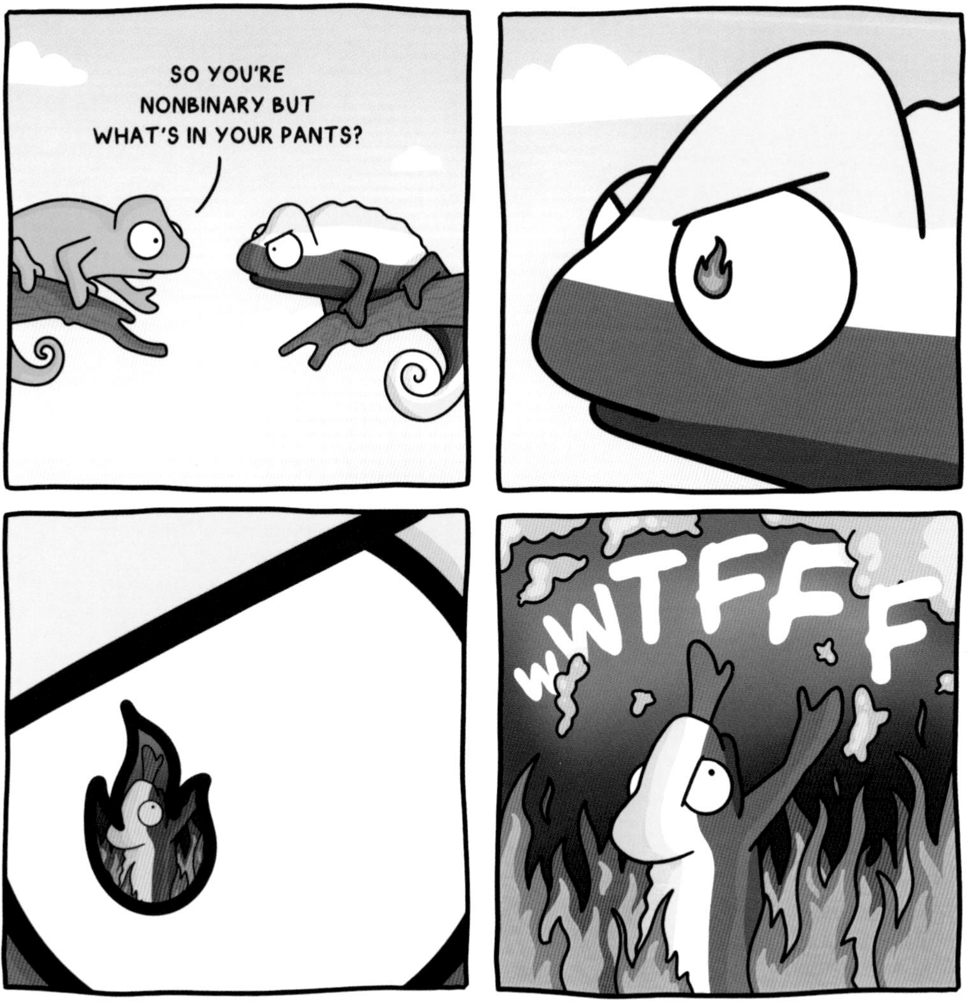
SO YOU'RE NONBINARY BUT WHAT'S IN YOUR PANTS?
wWTFFF

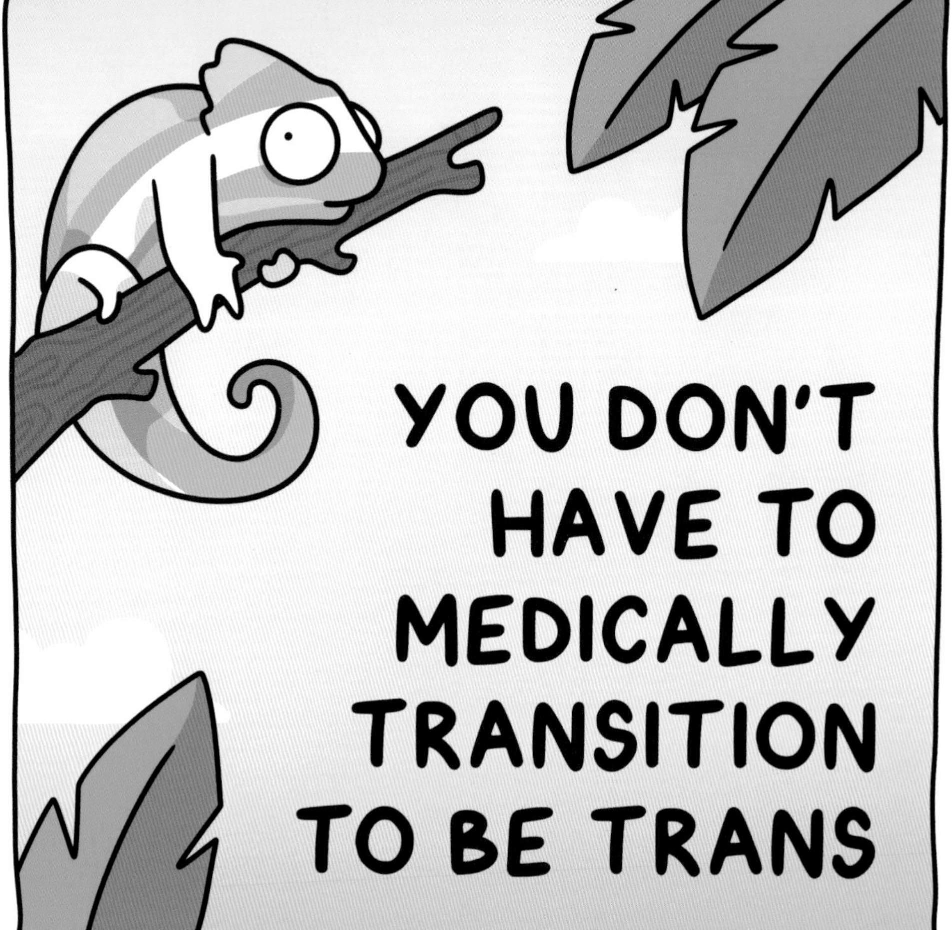
YOU DON'T
HAVE TO
MEDICALLY
TRANSITION
TO BE TRANS

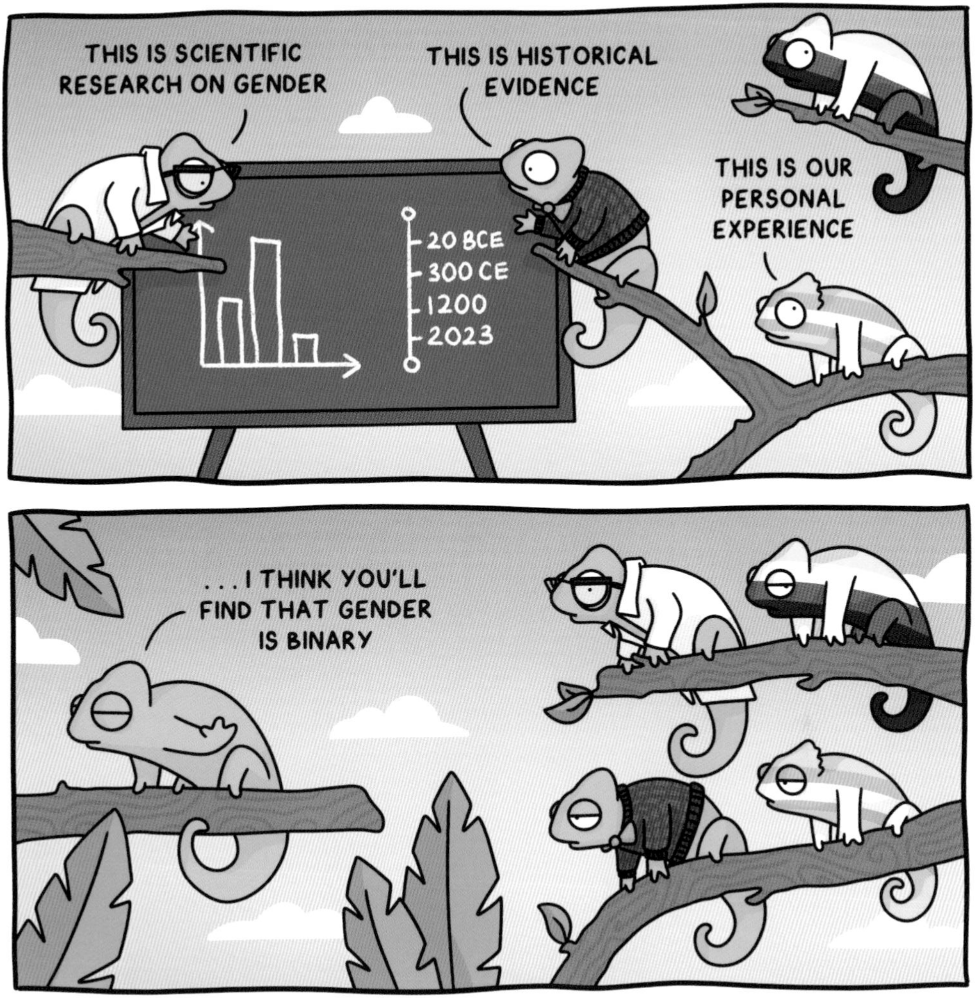
THIS IS SCIENTIFIC RESEARCH ON GENDER
THIS IS HISTORICAL EVIDENCE
20 BCE
300 CE
1200
2023
THIS IS OUR PERSONAL EXPERIENCE
. . . I THINK YOU'LL FIND THAT GENDER IS BINARY

PLEASE SELECT FROM
THE OPTIONS BELOW:
MALE
FEMALE

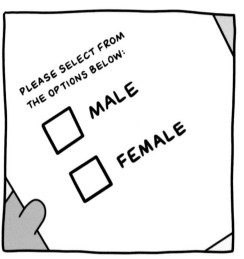

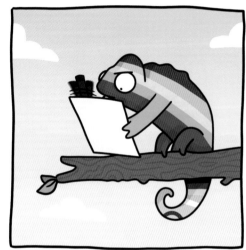

EASE SELECT
E OPTIONS BELOW:
MALE
FEMALE
GENDER IS A COMPLEX, BEAUTIFUL AND FLUID SPECTRUM THAT EXISTS OUTSIDE BOXES CREATED BY SOCIETY

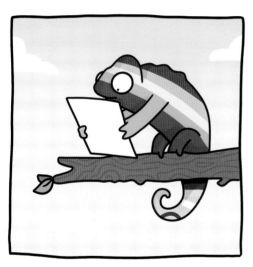

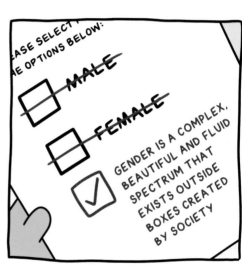

CHAPTER 6

LISTEN UP

Reminders, affirmations and words of wisdom
for you, allies and anyone who'll listen

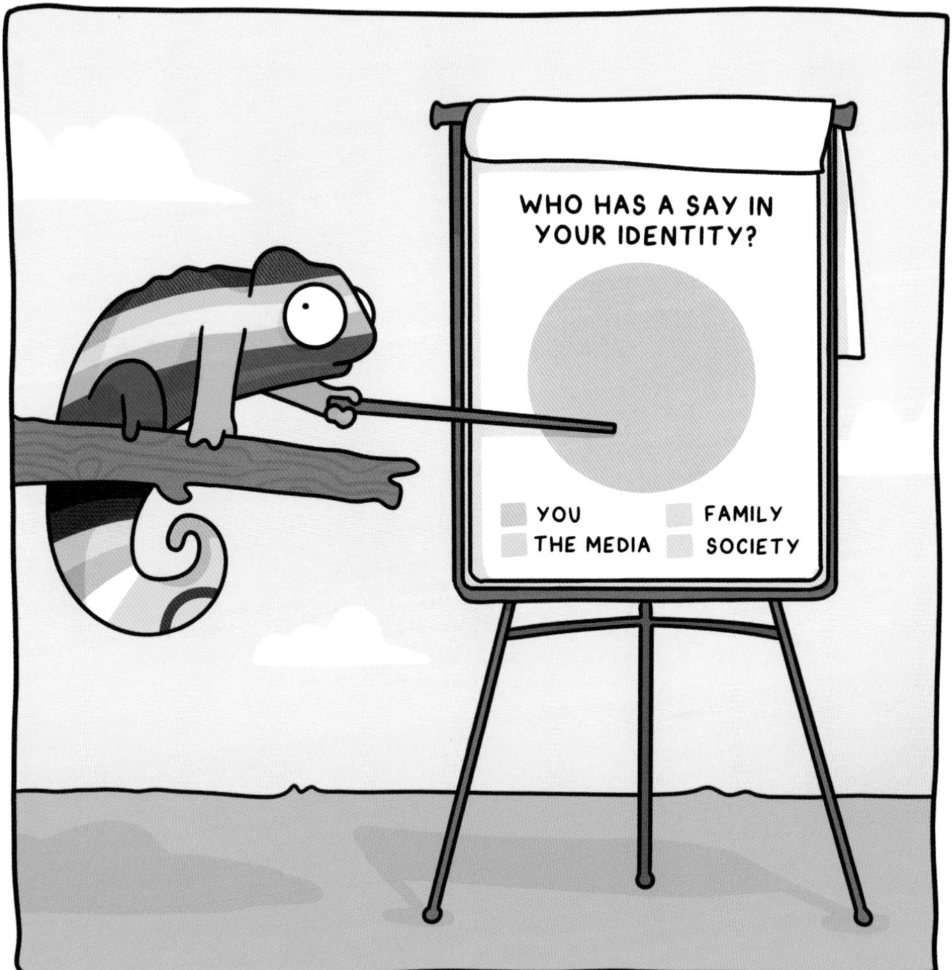
WHO HAS A SAY IN YOUR IDENTITY?
YOU
FAMILY
THE MEDIA
SOCIETY

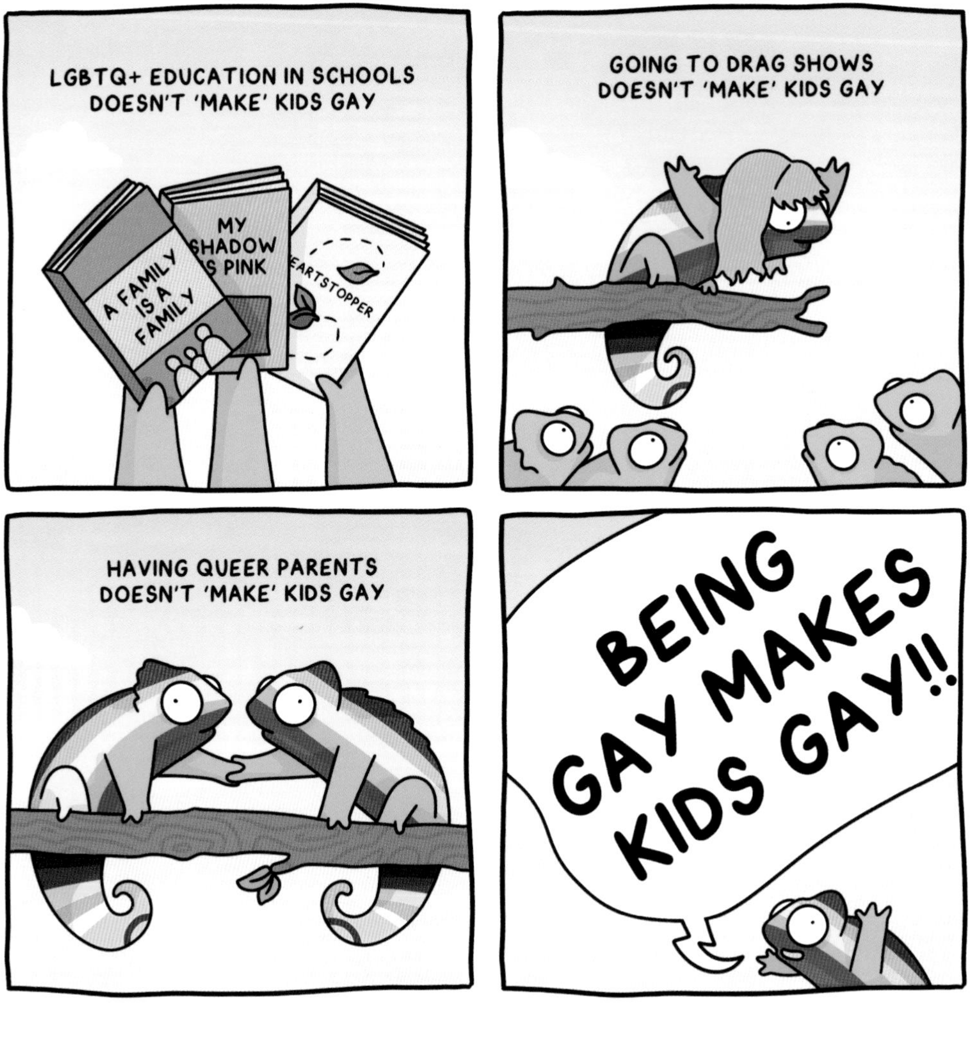
LGBTQ+ EDUCATION IN SCHOOLS DOESN'T 'MAKE' KIDS GAY
A FAMILY IS A FAMILY
MY SHADOW IS PINK
HEARTSTOPPER
GOING TO DRAG SHOWS DOESN'T 'MAKE' KIDS GAY
HAVING QUEER PARENTS DOESN'T 'MAKE' KIDS GAY
BEING GAY MAKES KIDS GAY!!

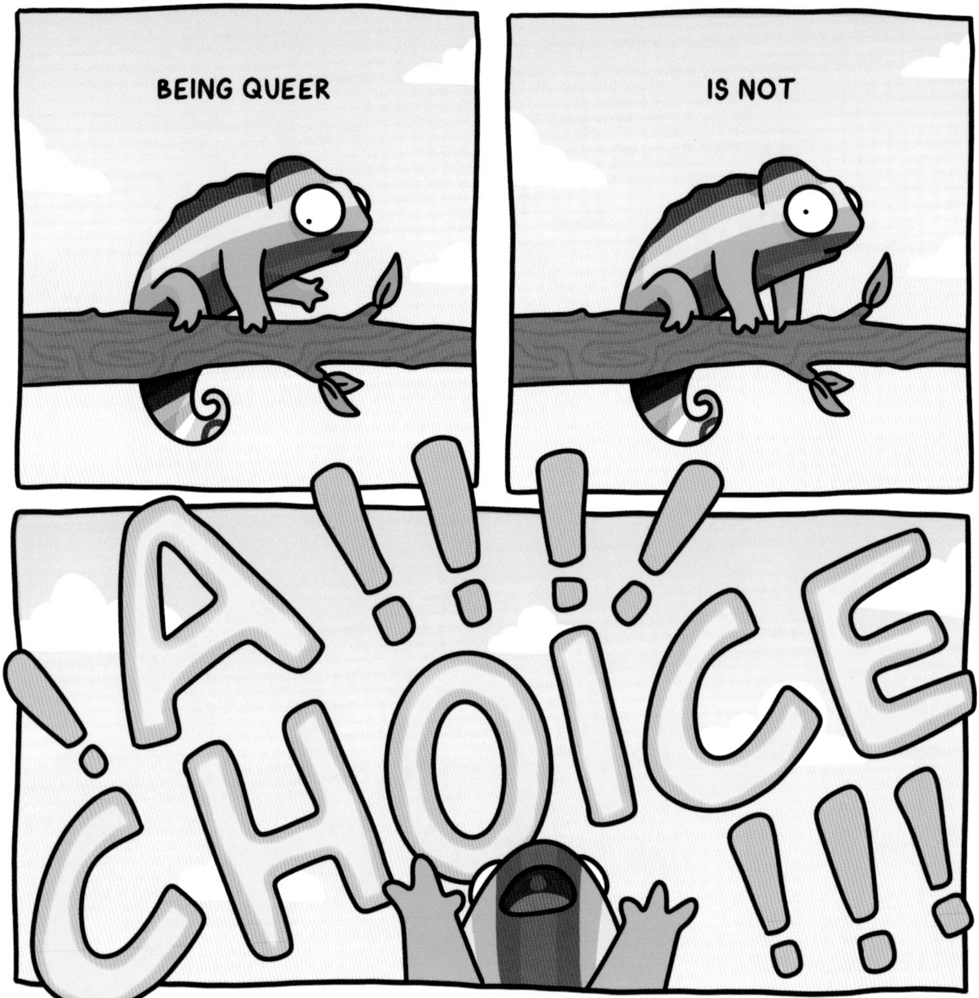
BEING QUEER
IS NOT
A!!!!
CHOICE!!!!

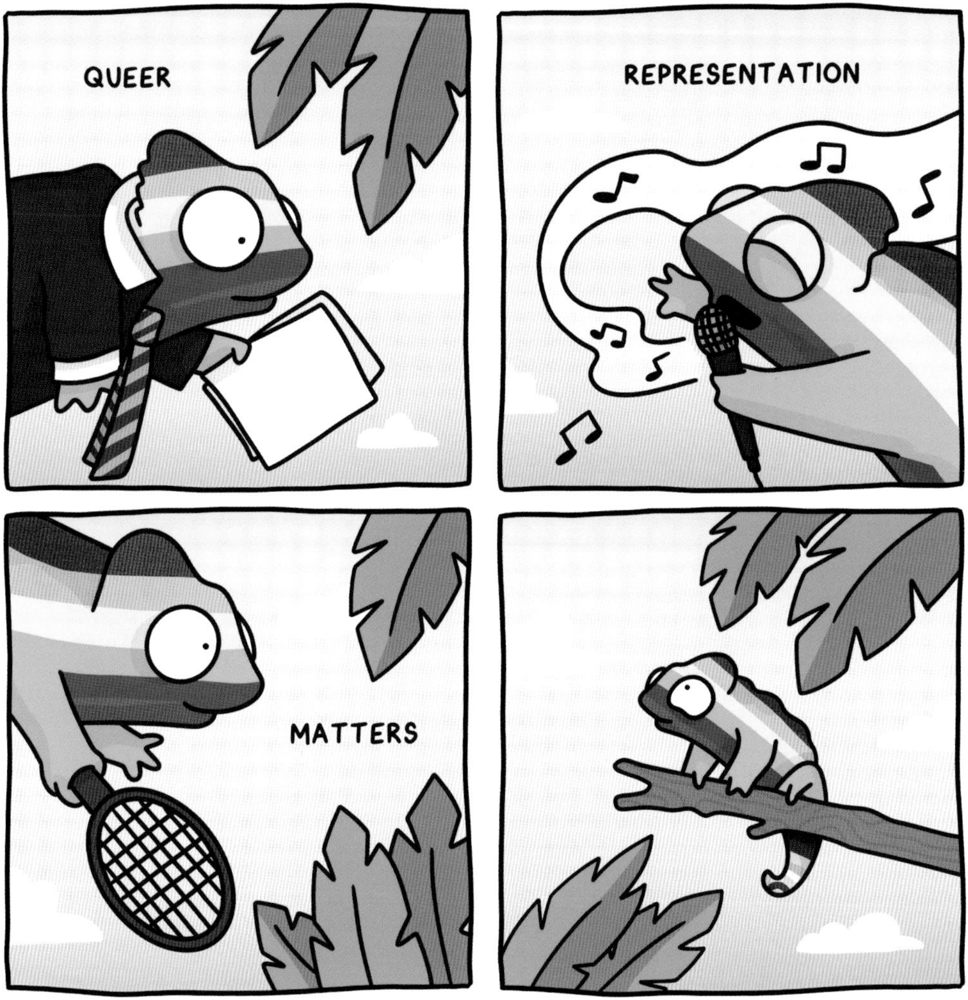
QUEER
REPRESENTATION
MATTERS

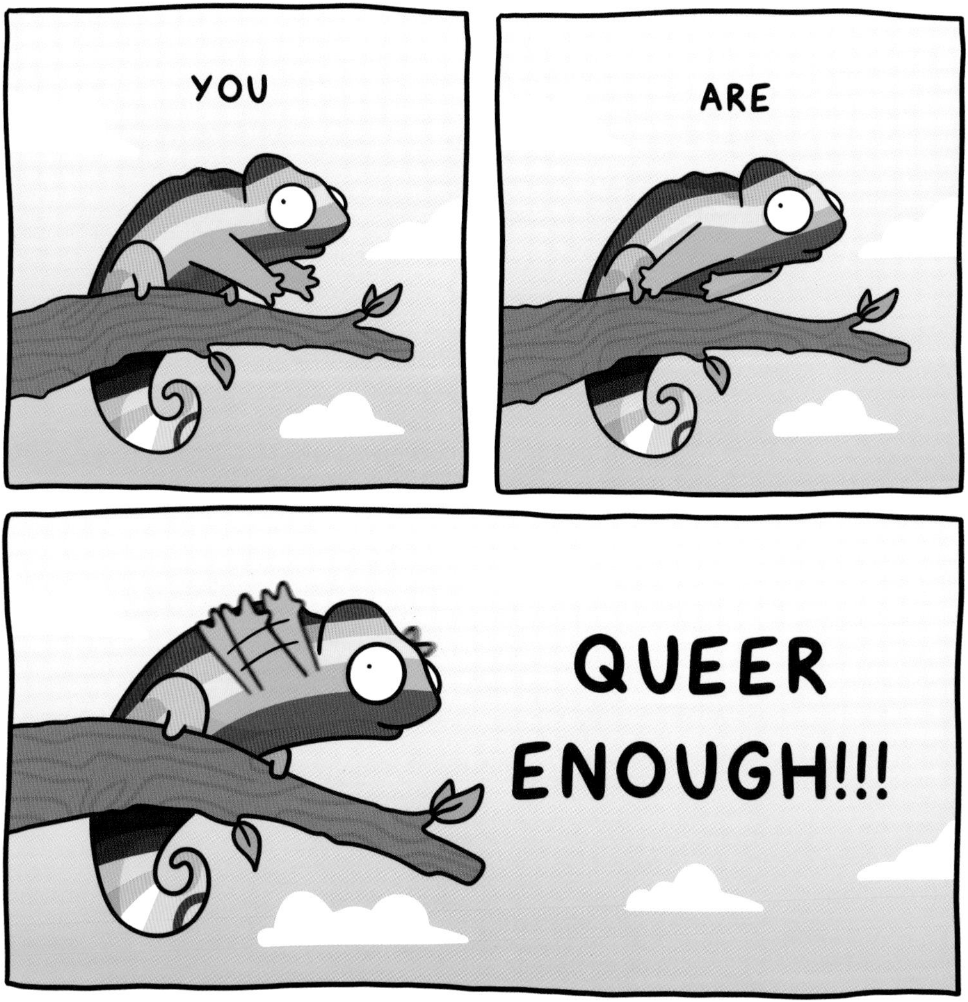
YOU
ARE
QUEER
ENOUGH!!!

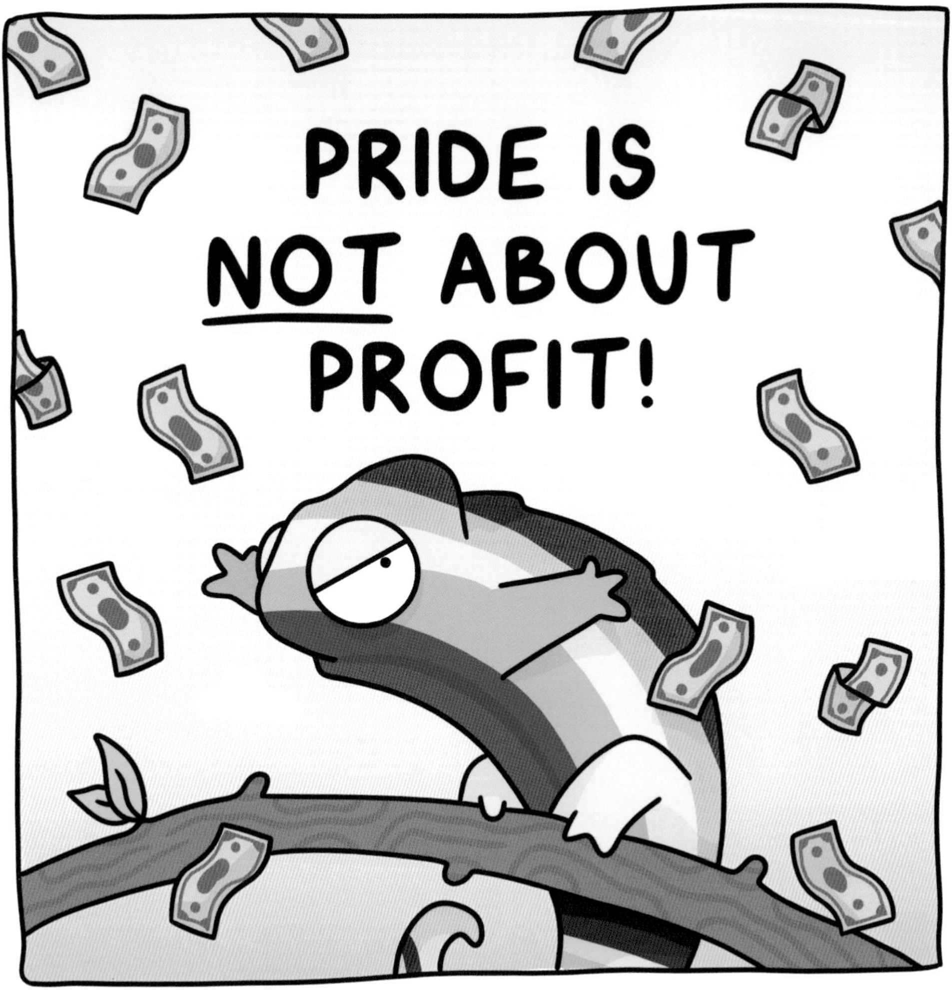
PRIDE IS NOT ABOUT PROFIT!

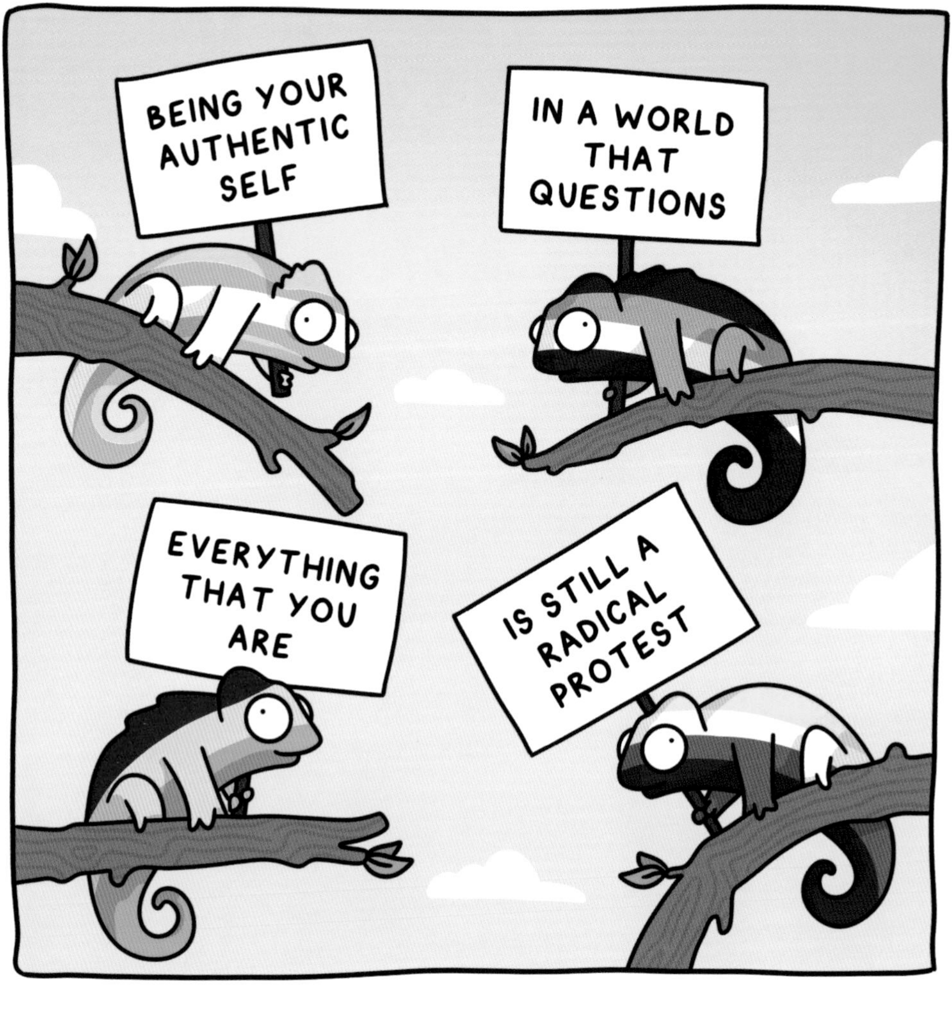
BEING YOUR AUTHENTIC SELF
IN A WORLD THAT QUESTIONS
EVERYTHING THAT YOU ARE
IS STILL A RADICAL PROTEST

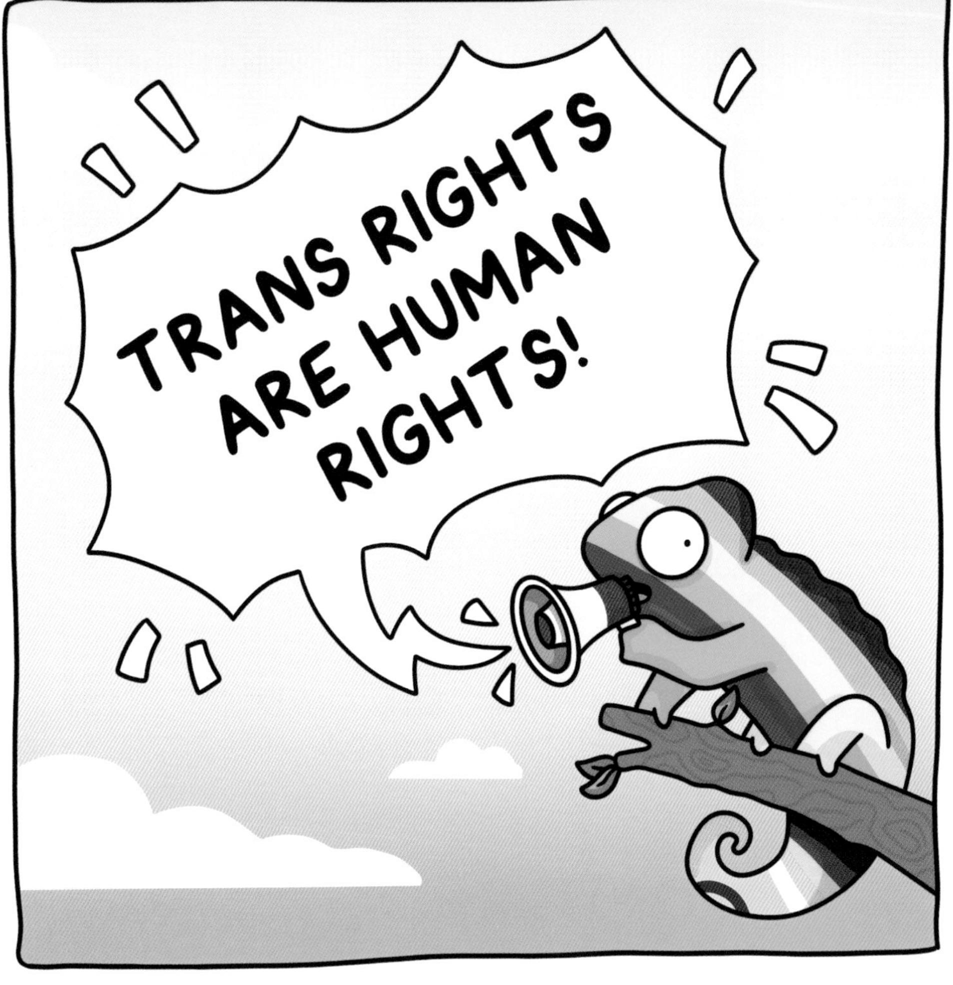
TRANS RIGHTS ARE HUMAN RIGHTS!

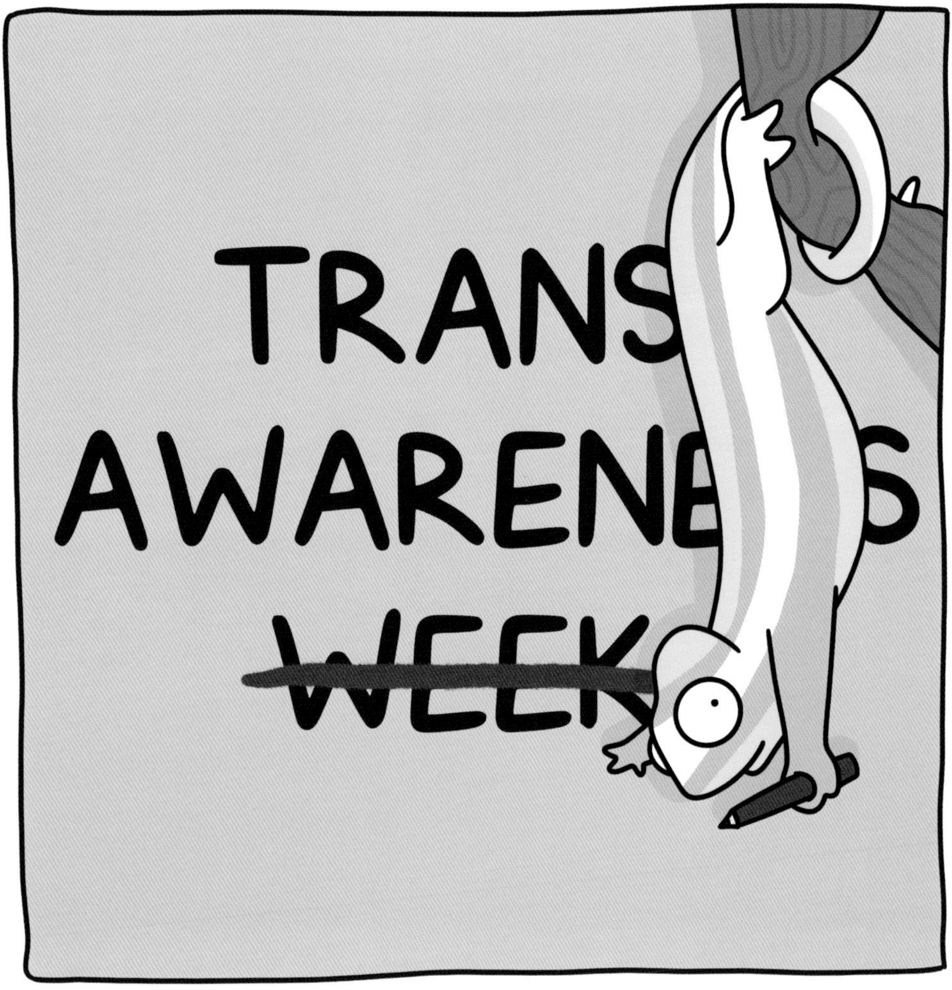
TRANS
AWARENESS
WEEK

4 WAYS TO BE AN ALLY

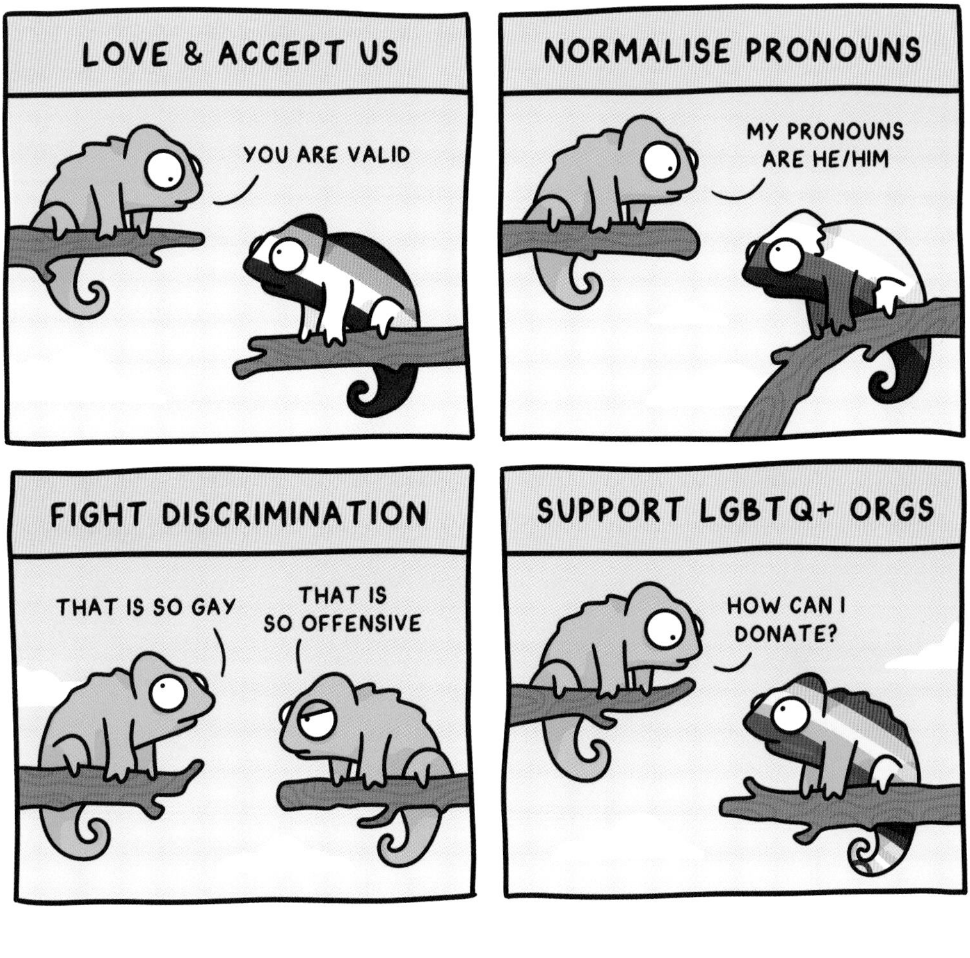

LOVE & ACCEPT US
YOU ARE VALID
NORMALISE PRONOUNS
MY PRONOUNS ARE HE/HIM
FIGHT DISCRIMINATION
THAT IS SO GAY
THAT IS SO OFFENSIVE
SUPPORT LGBTQ+ ORGS
HOW CAN I DONATE?

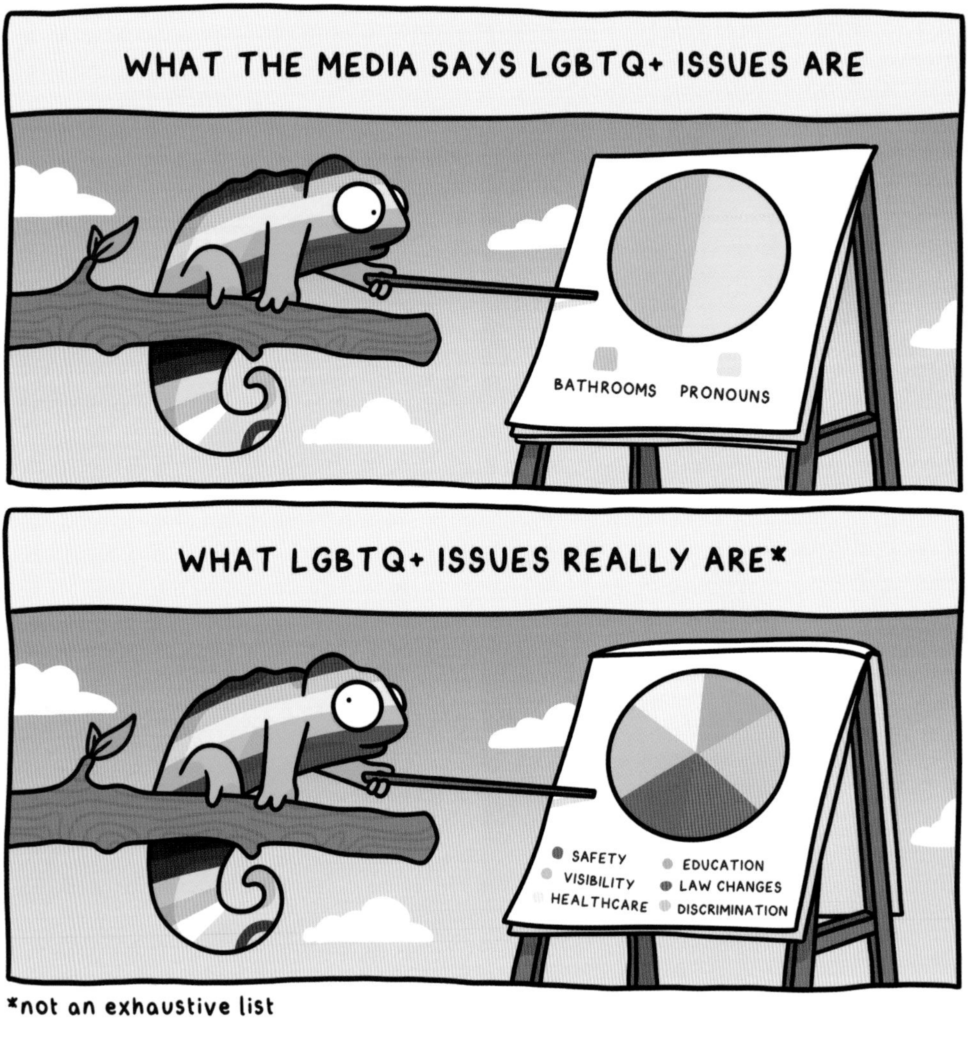
WHAT THE MEDIA SAYS LGBTQ+ ISSUES ARE
BATHROOMS
PRONOUNS
WHAT LGBTQ+ ISSUES REALLY ARE*
SAFETY
VISIBILITY
HEALTHCARE
EDUCATION
LAW CHANGES
DISCRIMINATION

*not an exhaustive list

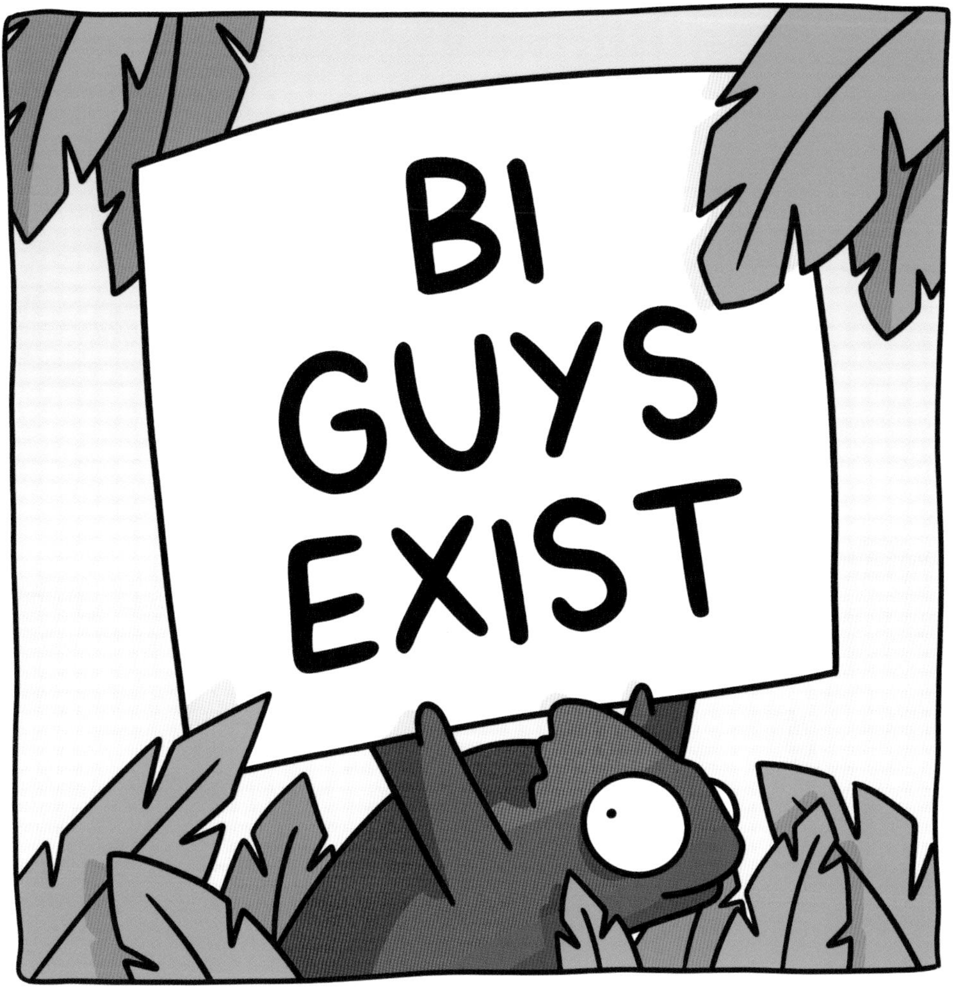
BI
GUYS
EXIST

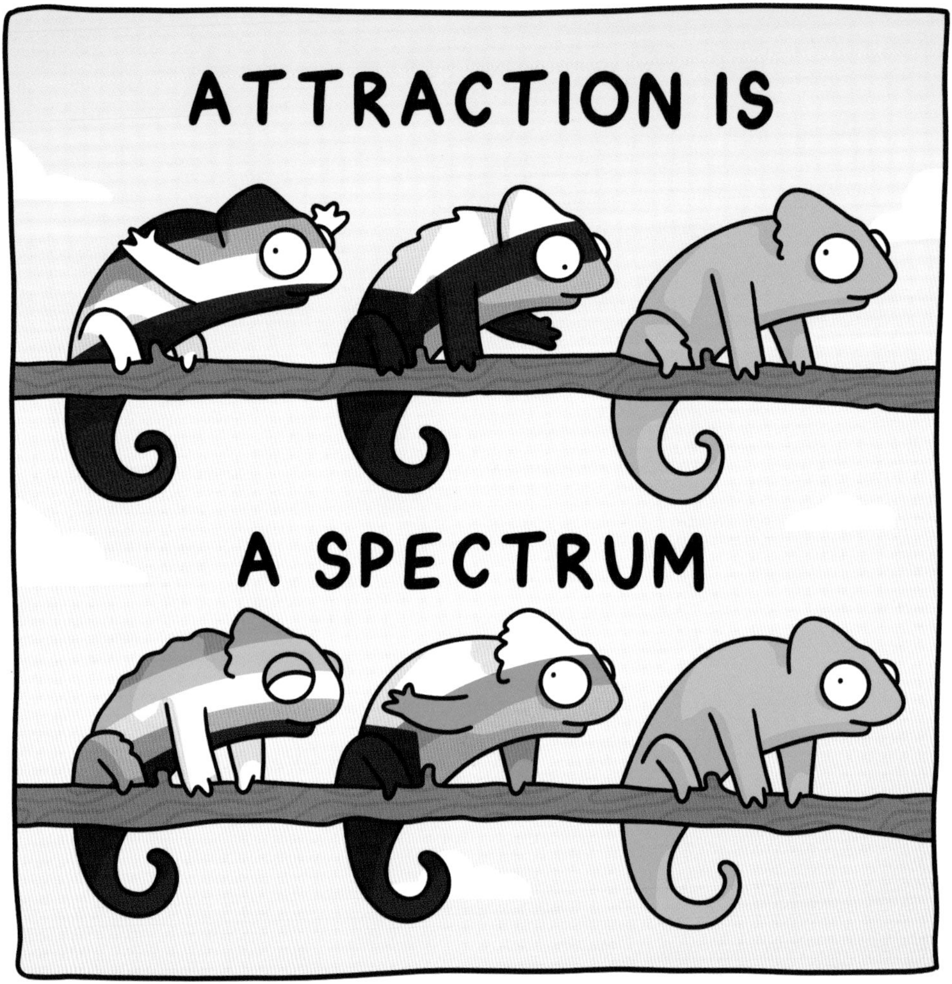
ATTRACTION IS
A SPECTRUM

WE DESERVE

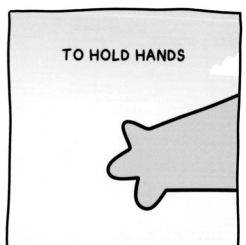

TO HOLD HANDS

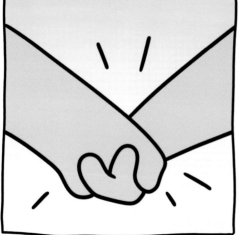

WITHOUT FEAR

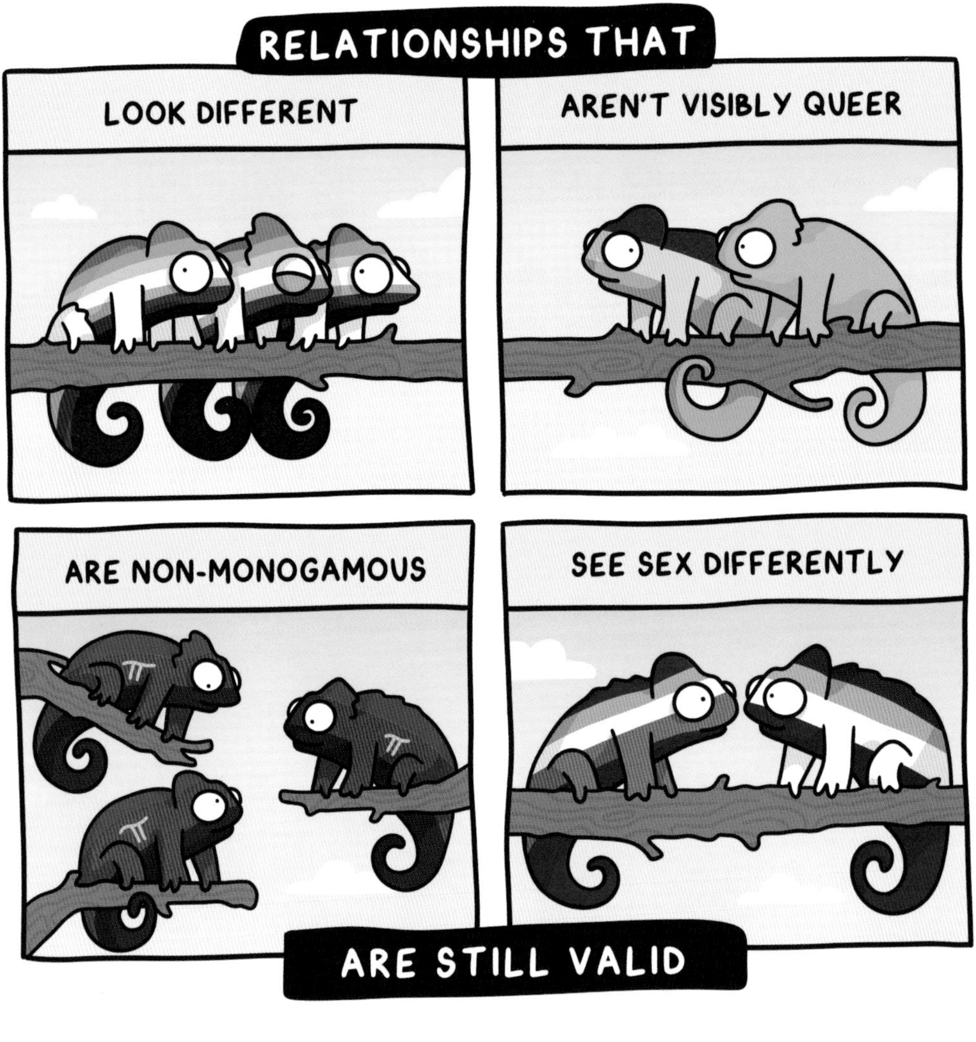

RELATIONSHIPS THAT
LOOK DIFFERENT
AREN'T VISIBLY QUEER
ARE NON-MONOGAMOUS
SEE SEX DIFFERENTLY
ARE STILL VALID

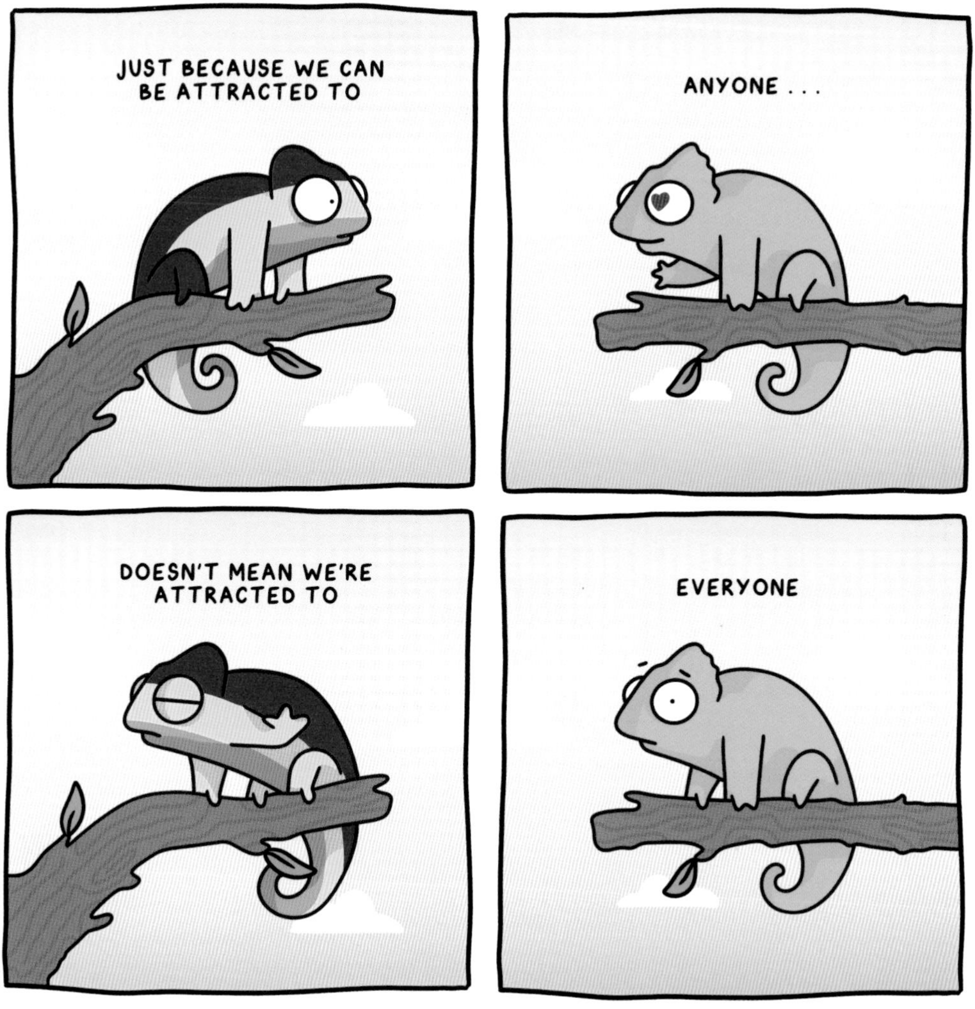
JUST BECAUSE WE CAN BE ATTRACTED TO
ANYONE . . .
DOESN'T MEAN WE'RE ATTRACTED TO
EVERYONE

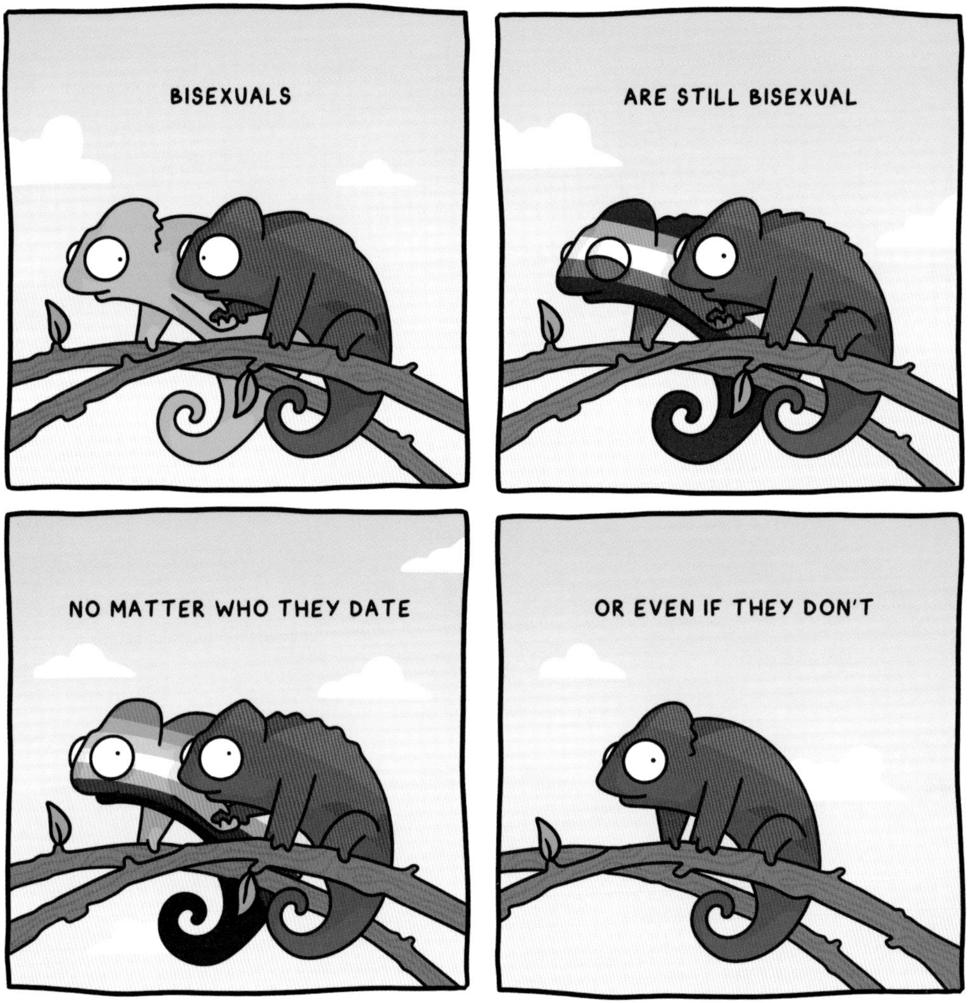
BISEXUALS
ARE STILL BISEXUAL
NO MATTER WHO THEY DATE
OR EVEN IF THEY DON'T

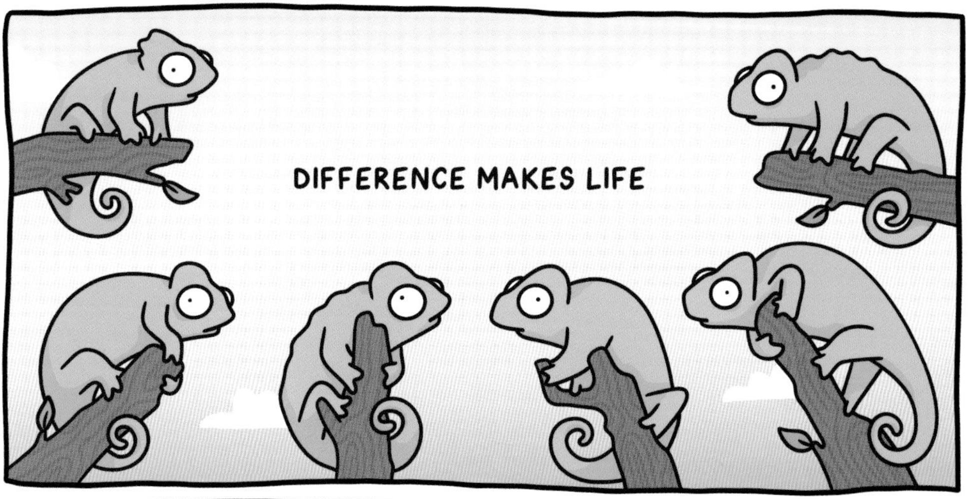
DIFFERENCE MAKES LIFE

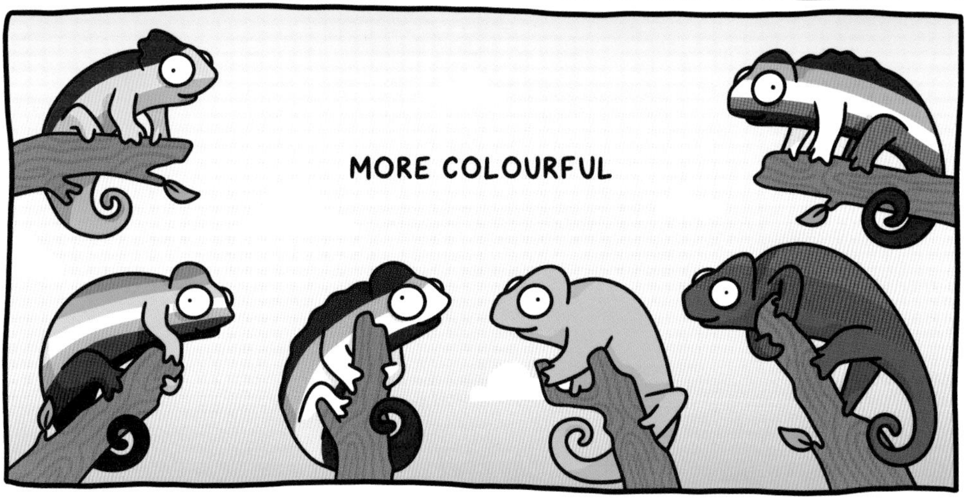
MORE COLOURFUL

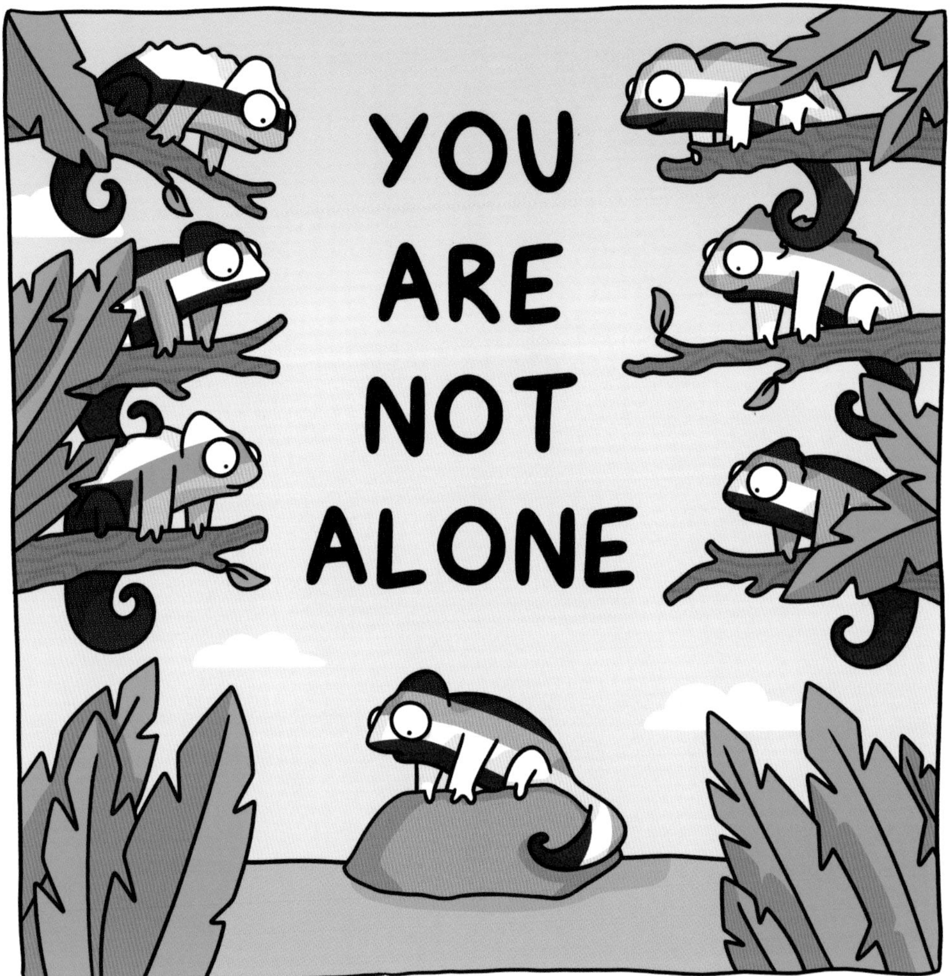
YOU
ARE
NOT
ALONE

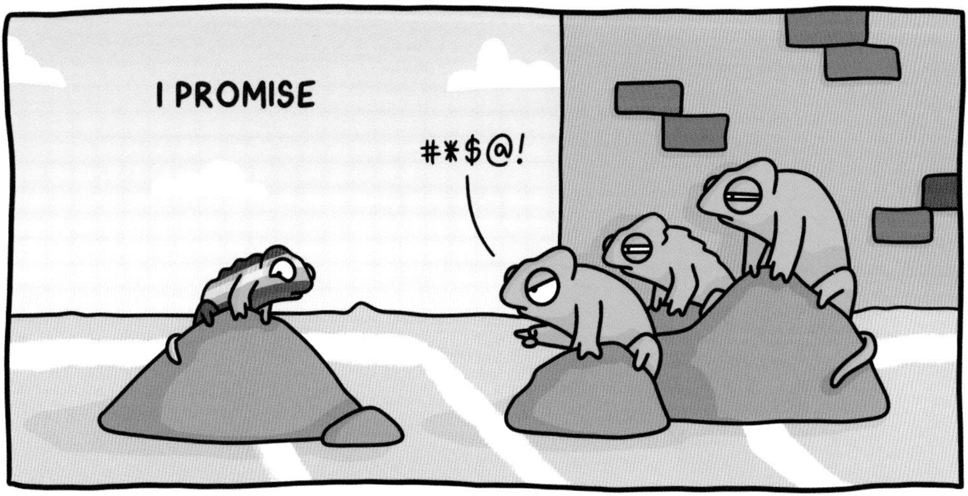
I PROMISE
#*$@!

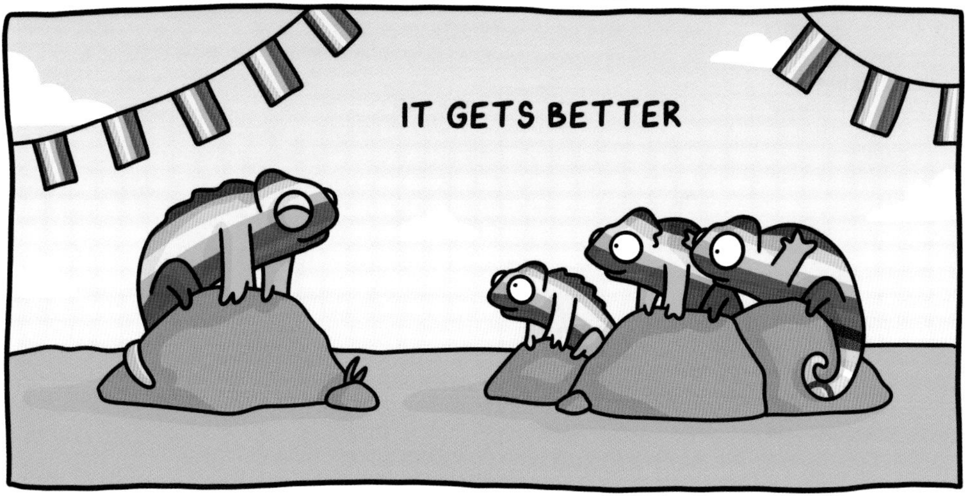
IT GETS BETTER

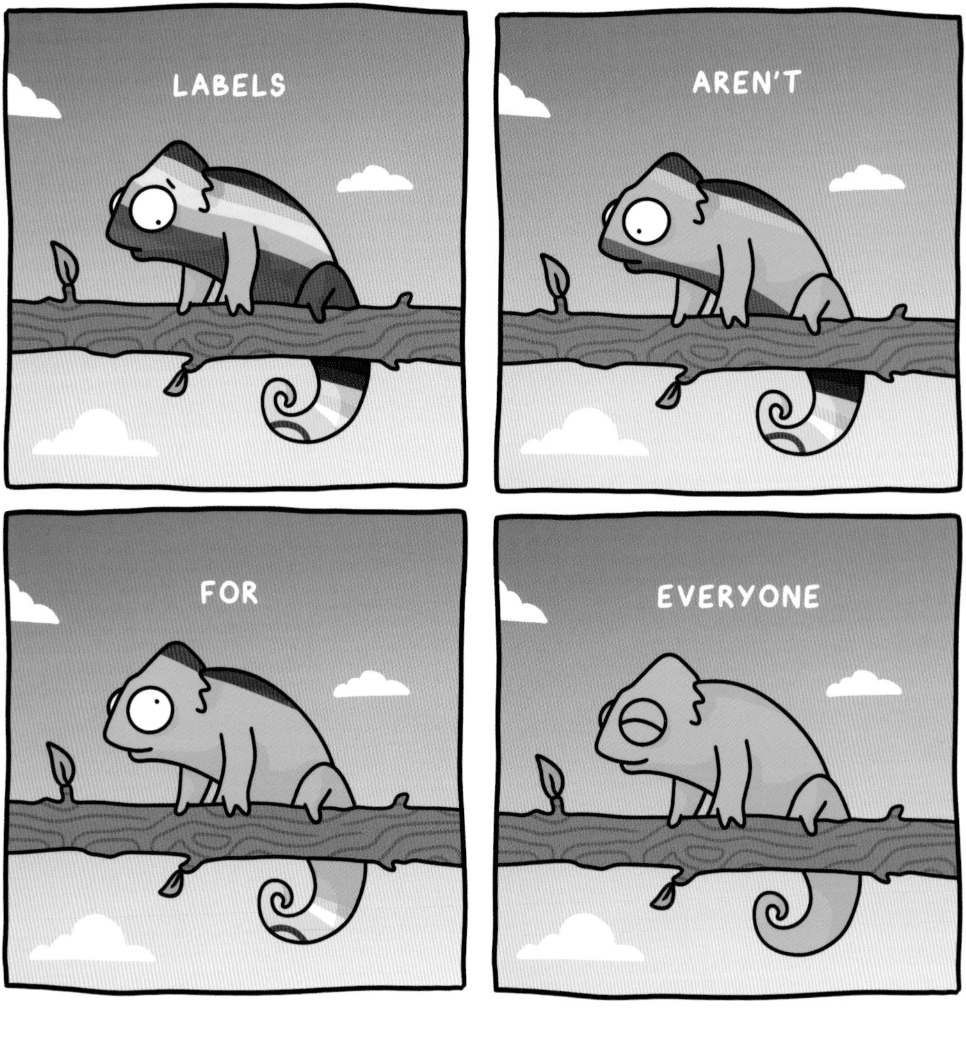
LABELS
AREN'T
FOR
EVERYONE

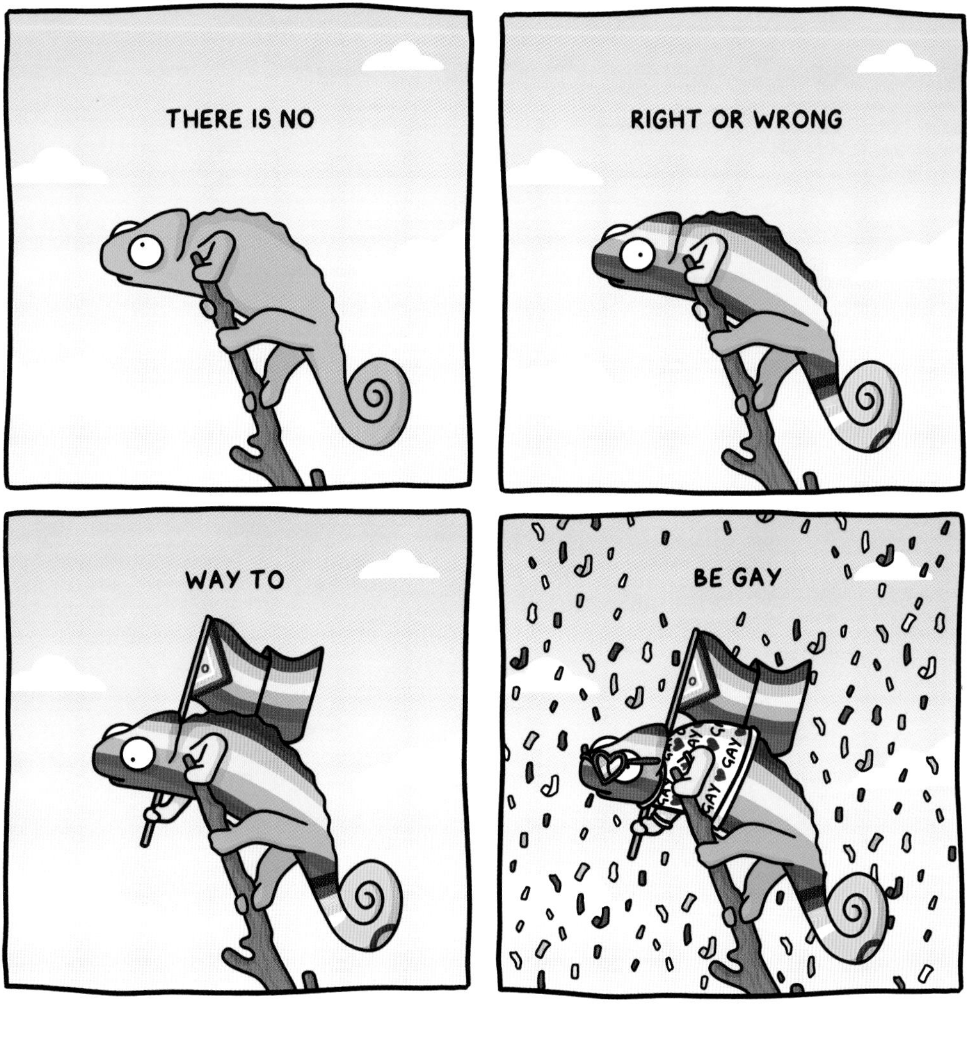
THERE IS NO
RIGHT OR WRONG
WAY TO
BE GAY

RESOURCES
& THANKS

Sometimes we need a little help, so here's a few resources for when you need them. I've included some Australian and international links, but it's always good to seek out local support that works for you. If you have other helpful suggestions, feel free to share them with me on Insta and/or TikTok **@QueeeerChameleon**.

AUSTRALIA

Urgent help (24/7 phone services)

Lifeline: 13 11 14

Kids Helpline: 1800 551 800

LGBTIQ+ Health Australia

lgbtiqhealthaustralia.org.au

LGBTIQ+ Health Australia delivers a number of programs and resources to help LGBTQ+ people manage their health and access inclusive health services.

Minus18

minus18.org.au

Resources for Australia's LGBTQ+ youth (18 and under).

QLife

qlife.org.au

QLife provides anonymous and free LGBTQ+ peer support and referrals for people in Australia wanting to talk about sexuality, identity, gender, bodies, feelings or relationships.

ReachOut

au.reachout.com

A safe place for anyone under 25 to chat anonymously, get support and feel better.

Trans Pride Australia

transprideaustralia.org.au

Trans Pride Australia has created several supportive online spaces for trans and gender diverse individuals, family, friends and allies to connect with others.

Twenty10 (NSW Only)

twenty10.org.au

Twenty10's specialised staff and volunteers offer free and confidential support, information and referrals to LGBTQ+ people of all ages, their families, professionals and communities across NSW.

GLOBAL

stonewall.org.uk

straightforequality.org

glaad.org

pflag.org

lgbtqia.fandom.com/wiki

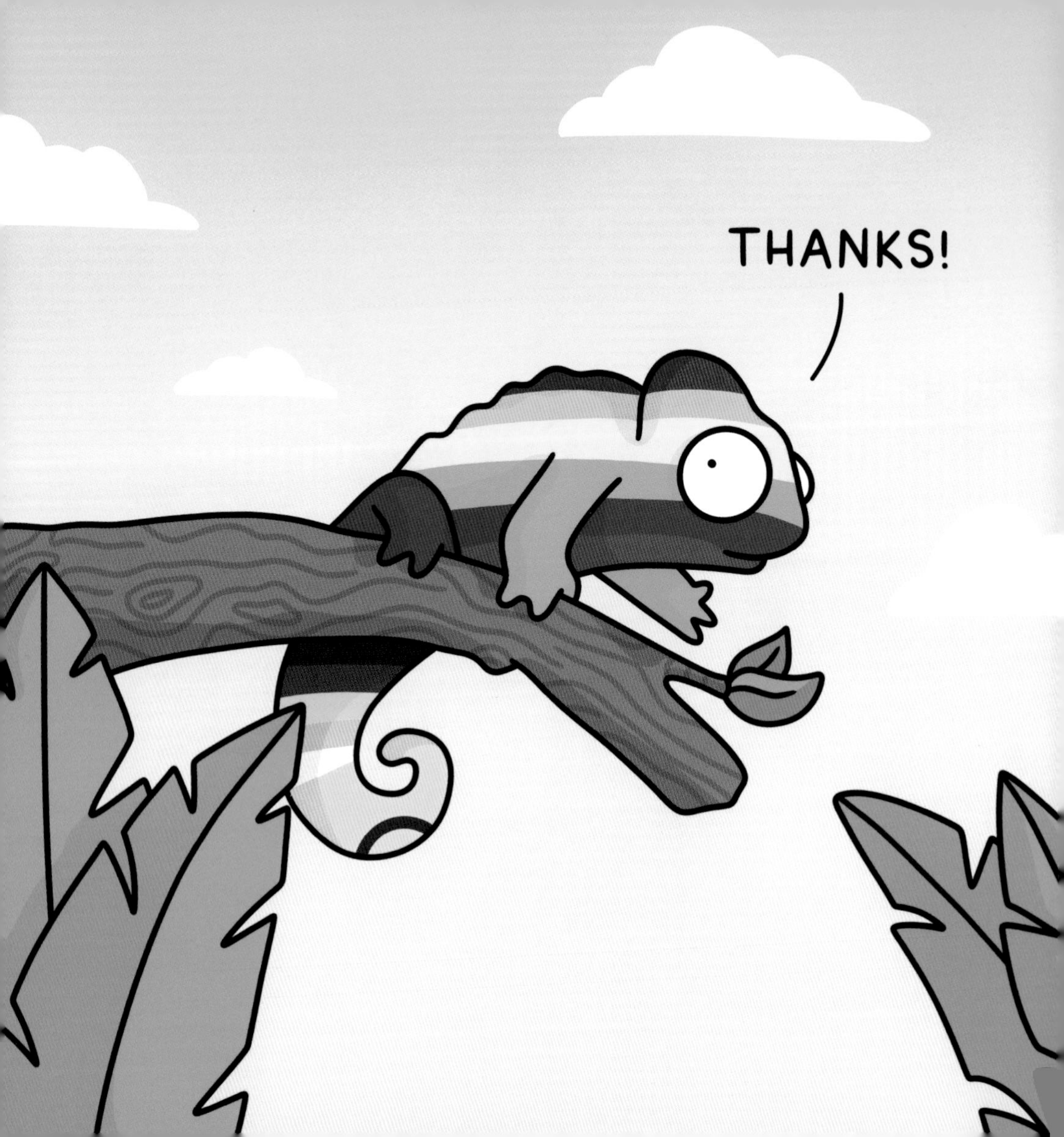
THANKS!

This book wouldn't exist without all the people who helped bring it to life along the way. So, it's time to say some massive thanks and all that jazz!

Izzy and the wonderful folks at Penguin Random House. Thank you for stumbling across our little corner of the internet and seeing the potential in the idea. Thank you for taking Queer Chameleon from pixels to paper!

Mum, Dad, for never questioning my random career moves and spontaneous hobbies and ideas, even when you didn't understand them. Thank you for never letting me give up on being creative. And Leigh, I have always been so lucky to have a gay twin brother who understands who I am. Thanks for being my biggest fan.

Lola. My true partner in crime. Thank you for listening to my constant 2 am ramblings when ideas popped into my head. And for being my muse . . . *cough*Lesbian Party*cough*. Thanks for being so patient, generous and gosh darn supportive. And for always believing in me when I didn't believe in myself. You da best.

Lastly, thank YOU! That's right. You who happens to be holding this book in your hands right now. Whether this is the first time we've met or you've been following along online for a while, you are making this possible and your support means everything!

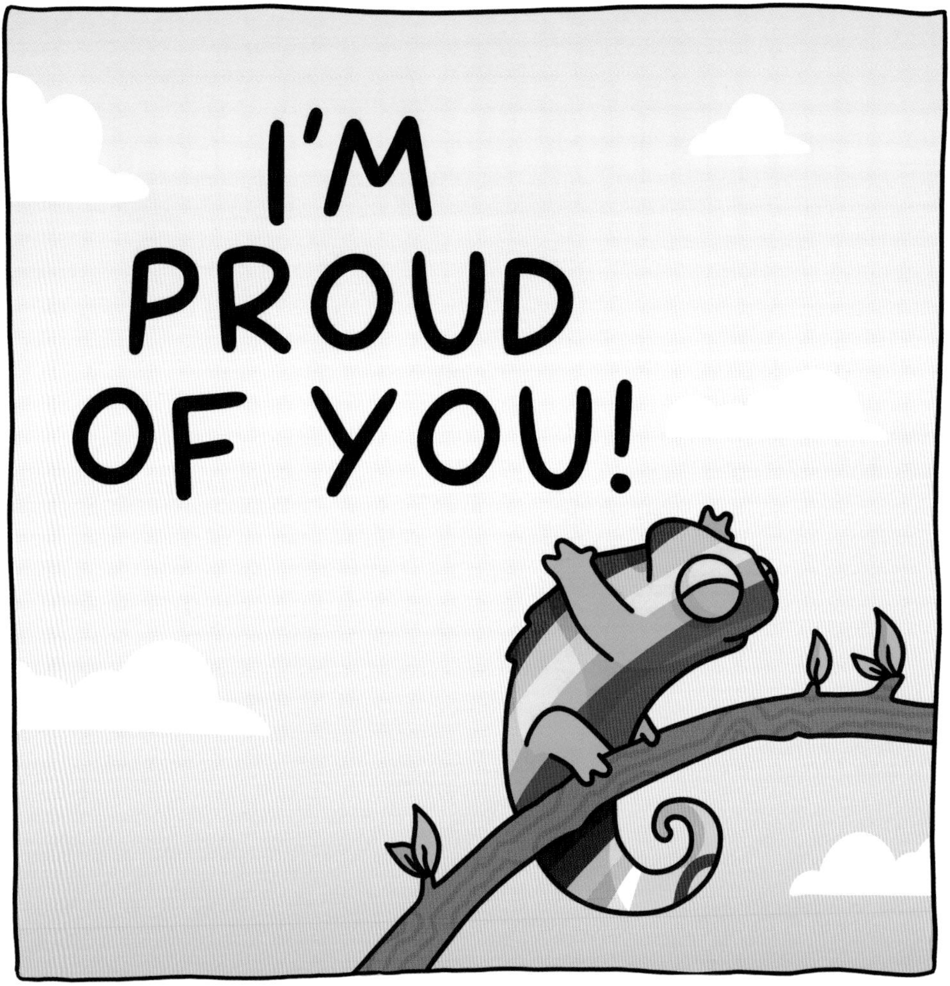
I'M PROUD OF YOU!

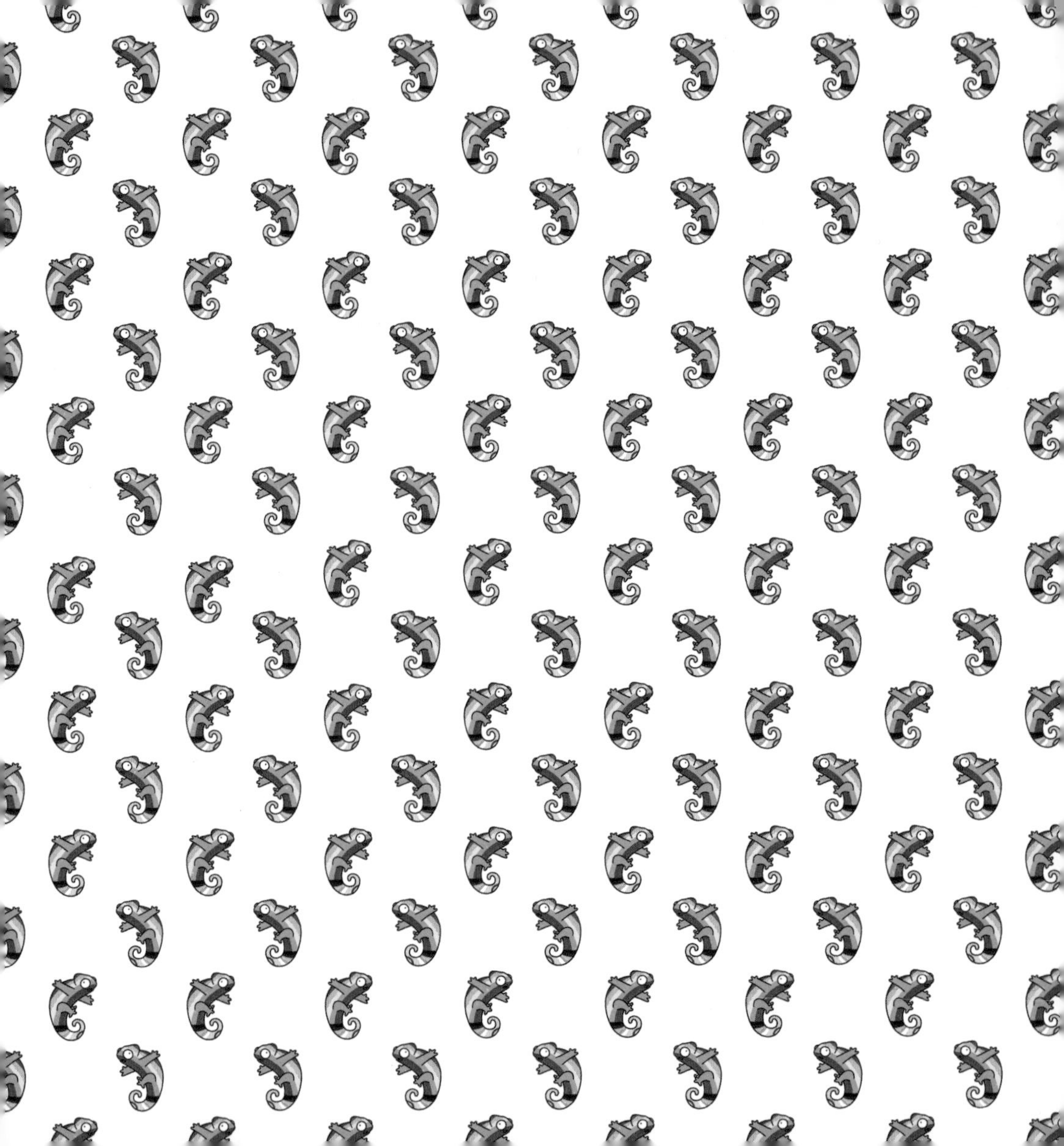